C000205428

Newbury

History and Guide

Susan Tolman

ALAN SUTTON PUBLISHING LIMITED

First published in the United Kingdom in 1994
Alan Sutton Publishing Ltd
Phoenix Mill · Far Thrupp · Stroud · Gloucestershire

First published in the United States of America in 1994
Alan Sutton Publishing Inc. · 83 Washington Street · Dover · NH 03820

Copyright © Susan Tolman, 1994

All rights reserved. No part of this publication may be reproduced, stored in
a retrieval system, or transmitted, in any form, or by any means, electronic,
mechanical, photocopying, recording or otherwise, without the prior
permission of the publishers and copyright holder.

British Library Cataloguing-in-Publication Data

A catalogue record for this book is available from the British Library.

ISBN 0–7509–0318–X

Library of Congress Cataloging-in-Publication Data applied for

Typeset in 9/11pt Times.
Typesetting and origination by
Alan Sutton Publishing Limited.
Printed in Great Britain by
Redwood Books, Trowbridge, Wiltshire.

Contents

CHAPTER ONE

Why Here?

N ewbury owes a lot to its geographical and hence its geological
position. The town now lies about 250 feet above sea level, and
the immediately surrounding district can be divided into two
geological formations with subsidiary strata: the chalk of the
Cretaceous period, and the sands and clays of the Eocene period.
The town's story starts about 100 million years ago when chalk
deposits, which still underlie much of the district, were laid
down beneath what is now believed to be the waters of a shallow, rather
than a deep, sea covering most of south-east England and eastwards across
northern Europe. At the end of this Cretaceous period (the latest system of
the Mesozoic era) – about 70 million years ago – the sea effectively drained
towards the south-east as earth movements slightly tilted the sea-bed. It is
the chalk escarpment, which extends from Calne in Wiltshire and passes
through Berkshire, which provides the main physical feature of the area.
Chalk is the underlying rock throughout the whole Newbury district and is
found at the surface north and south of Newbury. The lithological change
from bottom to top of the chalk formation means that there is underlying
Gault or Upper Greensand, followed by clay or sand and then the soft white
limestone called chalk. It is because chalk is a porous material that rainfall
permeates the chalk on the hills and is then prevented from escaping by the
Gault clay and the Reading and London clays.

Within the chalk escarpment there are remains of a lower parallel ridge
made by the overlying Eocene strata – the results of which can be seen at
nearby Cold Ash. Earth movements during the Eocene period brought about
subsidence of the chalk in two areas, one centred around London (including
Berkshire) and the other in Hampshire. As the sea returned, beds of sand
and clay – the Reading beds, the London clay, and the Bagshot and
Bracklesham beds – were deposited into its shallow waters. Sea water
covered the area, more like a great estuary than an open sea. The Reading
beds consist of mottled, plastic clays and light-coloured sands with thin
bands of flint pebbles. They are thinnest in the west of the district (at
Savernake Forest), at about 15 feet of plastic clay, and thickest at the east
near Reading, where they are made up of 30 to 50 feet of clay overlying 20
to 40 feet of sand. At Inkpen the London clay is 52 feet thick. Further earth
movements caused the London and Hampshire basins to separate into two,
each of which has been filled with clays and sands of the later Eocene
period.

It is thought that shocks from the birth of the Alps during the Miocene
period – about 15 million years ago – were probably responsible for the
London and Hampshire basins. But it was later movements which
effectively threw the Eocene and Cretaceous deposits into folds running

1

from west to east; it is the trough between two of these waves – now the Thames/Kennet Valley – which has determined the physical structure of the Newbury area. The town itself is therefore at a relatively low level and is underlaid with Eocene sands and clays.

About 2 million years ago saw the beginning of the Pleistocene period. Within that was the Ice Age, characterized by seven glacial periods and their intervening periods (known as inter-glacials), when the climate was warmer. Ice covered nearly the whole of Britain, but the Thames Valley is thought never to have been covered by permanent ice sheets. The last glacial period started about 45,000 years ago and these final ice sheets disappeared about 10,000 years ago. The climate began to improve enough for trees to grow again, but there is some debate as to whether this was the final glacial period or whether we are now living in yet another inter-glacial.

Archaeology has gone forward in leaps and bounds with the development of the radiocarbon dating method by Libby in the late 1940s. This, coupled with the fact that the current generation is more aware of its historical responsibilities, means that archaeological data is much more likely to be recorded accurately. Aerial photographs can show misleading cropmarks and now that archaeological evaluations must be carried out in areas of high potential before planning permission is granted, records are more reliable. Cropmarks are discolourations which could outline structures such as walls or ditches, pits or post-holes. However, cropmarks visible on aerial photographs have sometimes been caused by natural variations in the underlying clay/gravels.

Man arrived in this country quite early during the Pleistocene period. The journey was possible because Britain was connected to the continent by land bridges across the Channel and the North Sea. When the present A34 link was being built between the Robin Hood roundabout and the M4 in the mid-1970s, hippopotamus bones, dating from a warmer period before the Ice Age ended, were found. Red deer bones from the same period were also found and there have been many examples of Old Stone Age (Palaeolithic) implements being found around Newbury – at Wash Common, Boxford, Newbury station and Buckingham Road, Newbury. Any evidence of man being around Newbury at that time, however, is purely circumstantial since enormous flows of water caused by ice melting from the north disturbed the ground's surface. Other supposed Pleistocene forms – bones of horse, large-fossil ox and reindeer – were found at the old river terrace gravels at East Fields or St John's Road during the installation of drains in the town in 1894. The Old Stone Age or Palaeolithic period began 450,000 years ago. The Palaeolithic implements, which have been found in the Newbury area, could well have been deposited there when ice floes from the north began to melt at the end of the Ice Age.

The earliest record of man actually settling around here for a while – albeit staying in temporary camps, then moving on – is in Mesolithic (also known as the Middle Stone Age) times. Archaeological discoveries and research have clearly demonstrated the importance of the River Kennet between Hungerford and Thatcham throughout this period. Mesolithic man (this period covered from 8500 BC to 3500 BC) had much to adapt to – fewer herds of game, needing a more refined series of long-distance weapons, and the melting ice which gave rise to streams, lakes and swamps, which meant he developed canoes and weapons to catch fish. They are frequently called the 'hunter-fisher' folk. When the ice sheets melted around 6000 BC, the North Sea was formed and Britain became an island. Few sites in the Newbury district have proved more prolific in significant archaeological remains from a range of periods including Palaeolithic and Mesolithic than the old gravel pit at Enborne Gate. In addition, excavations at the Greenham Dairy Farm site, first discovered in 1894 during drainage work at Newbury pumping station next to the farm, revealed Mesolithic implements. It is not known whether an ancient gully, revealed during excavations at an abattoir there in 1963, was occupied for any length of time or just used as partial shelter. Excavations on sites in Bartholomew Street and Cheap Street, Newbury, in 1979 and 1981 respectively produced Mesolithic flints – the kind of find one would expect within a river valley area of Mesolithic activity.

However, by far the most important finds of the time in the Newbury area come from one of the few Mesolithic sites identified in Britain, originally discovered in the 1920s and further investigated in 1958–61 and again in 1989. Three archaeological sites in the Thatcham sewage works area – all within half a mile of each other – are related since they are all on a bluff of higher ground on the north side of the River Kennet. The Thatcham settlement was in a much more watery area than it is now. Modern archaeologists believe there would have been a whole series of river channels, not a single channel like today. Harold Peake, with Mr O. Crawford, originally recognized the site back in the 1920s. The settlement was woodland, dominated by pine and hazelnut trees, on the edge of the flood plain. Archaeologists say that the site was probably visited for months at a time over about 100 years in a semi-sedentary manner. They believe it

atcham sewage works,
ere a Mesolithic site has
en discovered

acted as a base camp, providing small bands of people with somewhere to return to when they had been away hunting. They lived on red deer, fish, waterfowl and wild fruit and vegetables, and transport would have been either on foot or by boat. Radiocarbon dates suggest the site is dated around 7800 BC. Archaeologists believe that the Kennet Valley in this period would have been an open marshy area, ideal for the 'hunter-fisher' folk.

In 1934, while excavating for a boating pool in Victoria Park (formerly known as The Marsh), Newbury, several Mesolithic implements resembling those found at the sewage outfall works at Thatcham were discovered. Their condition indicates that they had not been carried far and that the original settlement may have been within the borough.

Neolithic man was the first generation of farmers in Britain, as the development of agriculture swept across Europe. There have been several finds from Neolithic times made in the Newbury area – including pottery found at Enborne Gate Farm, Newbury, during gravel extraction, Neolithic weapons and tools and animal remains discovered during the town's drainage operations in 1894, and a handful of pieces of knapped flint, which may be of Neolithic date (about 2000 BC), from the site of a new housing estate at Dunstan Park, Thatcham, although no settlement site has been identified. In fact, settlements of the earlier Neolithic period (4200 BC–3500 BC) are elusive in Britain. In the south, houses of the later Neolithic period (3500 BC–2000 BC) are almost non-existent.

One of the most distinctive remains of the Neolithic period is the long barrow, a communal burial chamber. Earthen long barrows were followed by chambered tombs, to be used for successive burials over generations. The closest example of an earthen long barrow, and said by county council archaeologists to be the best preserved in the county, is at nearby Combe Gibbet, on the crest of Inkpen Hill. A gibbet, originally erected on top of the mound in 1676, has attracted visitors, and erosion along the spine of the mound has occurred. Protective works have now been undertaken. One of the main forms of chambered tombs was the gallery grave, commonly composed of megalithic uprights and roofing stones combined with drystone walling and usually covered by long barrows. The closest example to Newbury is the famous Wayland's Smithy near the Ridgeway in Oxfordshire. By halfway through the later Neolithic period, however, cremation was widespread, although burials were still carried out, only now under round barrows. Stone axes – an indication that people were passing through the area – have been found in the Kennet Valley in general, although not in Newbury or Thatcham in particular.

One group of people in the later Neolithic Age who had far-reaching consequences for man were the Beaker folk, named after the drinking vessels they popularized. One such beaker was found at Inkpen in 1935 and is now in Newbury Museum. The Beaker folk heralded a new phase – one where metalworking was introduced to Britain. But since stone remained the main material for weapons and tools, this phase has been assigned to the New Stone Age (Neolithic), rather than the forthcoming Bronze Age.

There is much evidence of Bronze Age activity in the Newbury area. By now, of course, metalworking was being developed, with new kinds of tools and weapons, including swords, being made. Although farming dominated Bronze Age life, other industries such as carpentry and metalwork were

Early Bronze Age (c. 2000 BC pottery beaker and bowl, foun at Inkpen in 1936

found in most settlements. Individual finds in the Newbury area include two flint axe-heads, thought to date from the earliest phase of the Bronze Age and held in store at Newbury Museum, which were found in the early 1870s at Bank's Farm, Thatcham, and fragments of a cinerary urn which were found in 1935 by workmen near Chandos Road. Chamberhouse Farm, Thatcham, was where, in 1991, about twenty pieces of broken pottery, thought to be late Bronze Age, were found on the flood plain close to the River Kennet. A ring-ditch, similar to many identified on the gravels of the Lower Kennet Valley and most probably representing a burial feature, was excavated at Lower Farm, Greenham, in 1990. An early or middle Bronze Age date was given to it from the collared urn pieces in the infill.

One of the largest discoveries of bronze implements in the area was found at Yattendon Park in 1878. Almost sixty pieces of bronze, including spears and tools, were found when the foundations for a new house were being dug. The date of the finds has been left to conjecture, except to say that since they were bronze it was probably before the Iron Age or the Roman invasion. Archaeological excavations in advance of residential development at Dunston Park, Thatcham, in the early 1990s, however, have shown the remains of a late Bronze Age settlement dating to around 800 BC. Work by Wessex Archaeology found the well-preserved remains of two round houses and ditches associated with field boundaries. The site is believed to have been a farm, with people growing crops and keeping animals. Rubbish pits contained storage and cooking pottery, and other remains show that cloth and metalworking both took place in the settlement.

In 700 BC the first iron-using culture in central and western Europe, originating from the Hallstatt village in Austria, reached Britain and iron gradually replaced bronze as the main material for tools and weapons. The main characteristic of Britain in the Iron Age was hillforts, a name used to describe a variety of earthworks – a term used to identify a fortified site defended by banks and ditches and enclosing small or large areas, many containing circular buildings. There are several hillforts close to Newbury, most notably at Beacon Hill, Highclere. However, archaeological remains from this period are few and far between, one reason being the comparatively short duration of the age.

Gold slaters coins, dated c. 50 BC, found near Hampstead Norreys near Newbury in 1979

CHAPTER TWO

In the Beginning

Although archaeological remains of the Iron Age period are scant, with only few clues left as to activity in the area, there is no doubt that there was a Roman presence around Newbury. Increasingly during the Iron Age, goods were imported into Britain from Europe as the Roman Empire expanded. The Roman invasion of AD 43 was the beginning of the end of the Iron Age in southern Britain, but the conquest was not completed in the north until AD 84. At the time of the invasion Britain was mainly a forested and agricultural country.

Roman roads were connections between garrison towns essential for the quick movement of troops and supplies, together with a network of subsidiary roads. Usually straight, they might change direction at prominent points. Silchester was a settlement of some significance in Roman times and a number of roads radiated from it. One of these went northwestwards to other main centres in the west – Gloucester and Bath – and that road forked near Wickham. In fact there has been speculation that the long-lost settlement of Spinae was probably centred along this Roman road between Silchester and Speen. Two itineraries (written records of Roman roads), compiled at the end of the second century AD, listed the places important on the routes and the mileage between the towns, and included a place called Spinae. The mileages on the itineraries differ and one destination was missing, making it difficult to plot where Spinae was. It is generally supposed to have been at Speen, but it was a fairly significant place and there has never been any record of sufficient archaeological material to support this, although from its name it would appear to represent Spinae. As far back as 1929 (W.E. Harris, Newbury District Field Club) there have been suggestions that the long-lost Spinae may not be at Speen, as has been popularly believed, but may in fact be elsewhere, such as Thatcham. However, there has been no archaeological evidence for that either.

The Romans left behind several substantial signs of occupation in the Newbury area. One of the most important pieces of evidence of Roman occupation was a cemetery, which was discovered in 1856 when the town's railway goods yard was being built near the A34. A hundred skeletons, two glass bottles, one cinerary urn and various pieces of pottery were found – indicating that the cemetery had been used for both burials and cremations.

Another important find, in the late 1920s, was the Roman roadside settlement in Thatcham, adjacent to the present A4. Finds at the site, in Thatcham Newtown, included pottery fragments dating from about AD 120 and fragments of building stone. Also included were coins from the latter half of the third century and the first half of the fourth century. A Romano-British well was also discovered there in 1925. In it were found small pieces

Group of pots from the first and second century AD, found among Roman cemetery remains discovered in Newbury at the old railway yard in 1856

of brick and pottery and one coin, which could not have been issued before AD 337. Other Roman artefacts were found when a gas main was being laid in 1932 at Thatcham Newtown.

There have been many other Romano-British finds in the Newbury area. These include pieces of pottery (found in 1928 on a building site in Salcombe Road and later pieced together to form part of a food vessel); remains of a Roman villa (discovered in 1907 in a field on the south side of the main road leading out of Newbury to Enborne); and pottery pieces (discovered in 1991 at Chamberhouse Farm, Thatcham, before sand and gravel extraction). Prehistoric and medieval pottery was also found at Chamberhouse Farm, but the amount of Roman pottery recovered indicated an intensity of activity at that period. On the opposite side of the River Kennet to Chamberhouse Farm stands Lower Farm, Greenham. It was here that in 1987 a ditched field system, possibly from the Roman period, was found. A major phase of occupation in the early Roman period (first century AD) was confirmed by the presence of a large amount of Roman pottery. One of the most archaeologically rich sites in the area – at Enborne Gate Farm, Newbury – produced in the late 1980s a ditch believed to date from the Roman period. In 1907, immediately to the east of the site, the foundations of a substantial Roman building were discovered.

About 12 miles from Newbury – at Littlecote Park in Wiltshire – a Roman villa and mosaic have been found. The mosaic is first thought to have been discovered in 1727 and it was reproduced as a coloured engraving and an embroidery. But the mosaic is believed to have been destroyed by 1730 and its location lost. Rediscovered in 1977, the mosaic (of which 40 per cent had survived) has been restored as nearly as possible to its fourth-century form using original material and modern terracotta. Coins found in the structure contemporary with the laying of the mosaic suggest a date close to AD 360. The building where the mosaic was found was originally thought to have been a temple, but is now believed to have been the dining room of a Roman villa. A thirteen-year excavation at the site, ending in 1991, has revealed a series of domestic buildings from the second half of the first century to the early fourth century. The recovery of seventh-century pottery and bone implements imply a Saxon occupation after the late Roman period. Covering the Roman villa was an eleventh- to twelfth-century deserted village and finally a post-medieval house which was demolished around 1760.

Roman legions were recalled from Britain between 406 and 408 to defend Gaul, the Roman province of Gallia, against an invasion of barbarians (someone from outside the Roman Empire) from across the Rhine. After that the British faced the threat of a Saxon invasion alone and it was in 410 that the Emperor Honorius wrote to British cities telling them that they must now look after themselves (*Historical Atlas of Britain*, Book Club Associates and Grisewood and Dempsey Ltd, 1981). The Saxons came from Scandinavia and northern Germany and they spoke a Germanic language from which our own speech was born. It is not for nothing that the six hundred years which separate Roman Britain from the Norman Conquest are commonly referred to as the Dark Ages, for there is a lack of historical information about the period.

Newbury appears to have been a planned medieval town, and anything before that is just coincidental since archaeologists say there is no evidence

The Domesday Book entry for Ulvritone. (Reproduced from the facsimile of *Great Domesday Book* published by Alecto Historical Editions, London, at the invitation of the Public Record Office)

of Saxon activity in the town itself. In fact, one of the few relics from the Saxon period is a silver penny of Egbert (King of Wessex from 802 to 839), said to have been found in Cheap Street, Newbury. Analysis in the early 1970s of pottery from the town centre identified two broken pieces of pottery associated with the earlier centuries of the Saxon period (from the fifth century to the eighth century). This has been interpreted by archaeologists as being the kind of fragment which finds its way on to the fields with the manure from a settlement or farm. Earliest documentary evidence of St Mary the Virgin church at Speen is in 1079, when the *Ecclesiastical History of England and Normandy* by Ordericus Vitalis says that the church was given to the Priory of Aufay near Dieppe. It was the Saxons who introduced the open field system of farming, whereby farmers had strips of land (each of about one acre) scattered throughout large fields.

It has long been suspected, and indeed believed, in many quarters that the long-lost Saxon settlement of Ulvritone, referred to in the Domesday Book, is Newbury. However, the evidence to support this is not firm, only circumstantial. At that time villages were grouped in administrative districts called hundreds, which formed regions within shires or counties. Ulvritone, although we may be uncertain of its exact location, is given in the book as being within the Thatcham Hundred. It was held by Ernulf de Hesding, had eleven villagers and eleven smallholders, two mills, a meadow, woodland and fifty-one plots of land. The book shows that the value of Ulvritone increased between 1066 and 1086 from £9 to £24 and this dramatic increase points to it being quite a large development.

In a 1972 publication of historian Walter Money's *History of Newbury*, originally published at the turn of the century, it is concluded that in the absence of materials to prove where the manor of Ulvritone was, it probably lay between Enborne and Greenham on the south side of the Kennet. Again, according to Walter Money, Ernulf de Hesding had forty-eight manors at the time of the Domesday survey. Ulvritone is said to be the only place in this district not accounted for and certainly appears to be the only place in Berkshire belonging to Ernulf de Hesding. The Domesday Book already tells us that Ernulf de Hesding held Ulvritone and we also know that a grant of William the Conqueror to the newly founded Abbey of St Pierre de Preaux in Normandy in about 1086 tells of 'the patronage of the Church of St Nicolas of Newbury' being given by Ernulf to the abbey. This then is the evidence supporting the theory that Ulvritone and Newbury are one and the same.

Newbury was, however, known by its present name a few years before the date of the survey, yet is not specifically mentioned by name. Chronicler

Ordericus Vitalis wrote in the *Ecclesiastical History of England and Normandy* that in 1079 the church of Speen was given, along with part of the rents revenue of Newbury, to the Priory of Aufay in France by Bernard, son of Geoffrey de Neuf Marche.

There are references in the Domesday Book to other places near Newbury, for example to Thatcham itself (thirty-five villagers, twelve smallholders, two mills, a church, valued at £30), to Greenham (eleven villagers, nineteen smallholders, a church, four slaves, one and a half mills, all valued at £6), to Donnington (four villagers, three smallholders, two slaves, a mill, valued at 70 shillings), to Shaw (four villagers, twelve smallholders, three slaves, one mill, valued at £6), to Speen (nine villagers, ten smallholders, a church, seven slaves, a mill, valued at £10) and several references to Enborne. The Domesday Book was compiled in 1086, twenty years after Duke William of Normandy (later crowned king) conquered England. Most of the lands of the English nobility were granted to his followers, effectively setting up the feudal system.

CHAPTER THREE

Medieval Newbury

T he name Newbury first appears in a document relating to the Priory of Aufay in the diocese of Rouen in 1079, at a time when there were often connections between Newbury and churches in this area of France. Newbury itself, once established, appears to have developed rapidly throughout the eleventh and twelfth centuries. Before the establishment of the settlement, the town was just open fields.

Earliest traces of activity in the Cheap Street/Bartholomew Street area are said to point to small-scale, almost light industrial use. Cheap Street in the very early twelfth century was low lying and the whole area was very soggy. A deliberate levelling up with the use of gravel then took place in both the Cheap Street and Bartholomew Street area, where modern pavement level is over a metre higher than the ground was when the town first started to develop. Before this building-up took place, the area was liable to flooding and so few traces have been found in archaeological digs of early post-built structures. However, once development began on street frontages in Cheap Street and Bartholomew Street (not shops as such, but probably domestic buildings with traders as occupants), there was a virtual continuous sequence of buildings running right through to the present day. Evidence of more formal buildings in Bartholomew Street at a slightly earlier stage than in Cheap Street suggests that this was probably considered a better street to live in. By the twelfth and thirteenth centuries, the Market Place area was beginning to be developed and a fragment of stone window moulding from around that date points to there having been quite a substantial stone building somewhere in that area at that time.

There has been much speculation about the existence of a twelfth-century Newbury Castle. Many public buildings have proudly displayed an image of the castle. In every case it has been portrayed as being made of stone blocks. One of them is the library, which still carries its carving above the original entrance in Cheap Street. A castle was the official badge or emblem of the borough in the seventeenth century and remained so until a new Coat of Arms was granted in 1947, which still incorporates a castle as its crest. Borough documents carried the mark of the castle and even town souvenirs displayed it. Local opinion even has it that the 'stone building' in the wharf is built from the castle's remains.

For many years it has been thought by Newbury residents, and indeed until relatively recently by archaeologists and historians too, that the castle site was in the wharf area. A survey in 1990 in advance of a proposed wharfside development, which has now been shelved, showed that Newbury Wharf was definitely not the site of a structural castle. Even the presence there of a 'motte and bailey' type castle was unlikely because the size of

Local legend says that this building at Newbury Wharf, now used by the Kennet and Avon Canal Trust, was built from the remains of Newbury Castle

Excavations in 1990 at Newbury Wharf in search of Newbury Castle

such a construction would have been evident and nothing was found. Suggestions have been made since the excavation that maybe the castle was further west than in the wharf area, somewhere closer to the Market Place.

In fact, the only real evidence for the existence of this castle is down to a documentary reference in a French journal to a Newbury castle being besieged in 1152–3, which could just as easily mean somewhere in the vicinity of the town. Accordingly, the castle may not be in the town itself at all. It was said that the castle was being held for Queen Matilda by John Marshal, when King Stephen's troops reached Newbury and took John Marshal's son William as a hostage. Later, William was created Earl of Pembroke and Great Protector and is said to have told his story to John Erleigh, who passed it on in a French poem.

Recent re-evaluation of the historical sources by Paul Cannon of Newbury District Museum concludes that the tradition of a stone-built castle surviving into the later Middle Ages is unsupportable myth and that if a castle did exist, it was most likely to have been earth and timber and short-lived. Mr Cannon also concluded that what has been written in the past about the castle 'consists of a mixture of fact, misinterpretation and error'. All we can be sure of is that there was a castle at Newbury involved in a siege during Stephen's reign.

Many writers, drawing heavily on Walter Money's work, have said that remains of Newbury Castle still existed into the seventeenth century. It has been claimed that an entry in the churchwarden's accounts of the parish church shows that timber from the castle was used to make an oak outer door for the church in 1626–7. But the Cloth Factory, sometimes known as the Castle or Hospital, was built in 1626 and it is possible that this is the building referred to by the churchwarden. A strict account of timber was kept and any surplus would have been sold. Other errors regarding the existence of the castle after the twelfth century have been made. One author appears to have confused the castle with an inn called 'The Castle' in a document in 1692. Hadcock, writing in 1979, said: 'at least a portion of the castle was occupied for habitation in 1692, as is shown by a rent for encroachment in the hands of the Borough Archivist.' But a study of the document, held at Berkshire Record Office, shows quite clearly that the property referred to is not a castle, but an inn which was fined five shillings for encroachment.

Medieval England consisted of small groups of people of up to several hundred in an agricultural-based community. Control and protection of many of these groups came from lords, who in return for certain duties gave them rights and privileges, and it is this manorial society which existed after the Conquest for several hundreds of years. During the Middle Ages there were none of the many functions of local government of today and the manor was more of an economic unit. A manor is effectively an area of land, a term for an estate, and does not necessarily imply the presence of a manor house. Administration was managed by the local lord's stewards and bailiffs and reviewed at their courts baron and courts leet, which administered a local law based on custom.

'Newbury Landmarks'. A twelve-view novelty postcard, *c.* 1920, with a representation of Newbury Castle on the front

The absence of a borough charter (whose function was originally to outline an economic unit, but from the late Middle Ages also recorded the grant of privileges by kings and lords) is not conclusive evidence of non-borough status, but conversely a charter does mean that a place was a medieval borough. Borough status brought with it the replacement of miscellaneous tolls and dues by a fixed payment by the whole borough, the right of burgesses to own and dispose of their property by sale or hereditary bequest and the right of burgesses to elect their own officials such as bailiffs and coroners. A burgess was a free man who, as long as he paid his rent, could dispose of his land as he wished and would not have to work for the lord of the manor. This freedom sometimes had the effect of drawing men to the towns.

No medieval charter has survived for Newbury, but other evidence – for example, an entry in the Pipe Rolls (accounts rendered by sheriffs to the Exchequer) of 1189 which refers to burgesses in Newbury – points to the town having borough status. Two burgesses were sent from Newbury to Edward I's (king from 1272 to 1307) parliament and three representatives were summoned to the 1317 conference on trade and manufacture, called by Edward III. As medieval times progressed, so did the burgesses' responsibilities and the costs of town maintenance – for example, maintenance of certain buildings and drainage of streets.

Newbury Manor was held by the Chaworth family in 1166 and from then onwards its descent became complex. In about 1217 it came into the hands of William Marshal, Earl of Pembroke, and after many changes of hands (including a spell from 1204 when King John took Newbury into his own hands in retaliation for the seizure of his property in Normandy), it returned in 1274 sub-divided to the female line of the Marshal family. Two members were sent to parliament by the borough in 1275. It was after 1316 that the Mortimer family obtained manorial rights in Newbury and in 1425, upon the death of Edmund Mortimer, Earl of March, Newbury passed to Edmund's nephew Richard, Duke of York.

It was the subsequent struggle between the houses of Lancaster and York for possession of the throne, known as the Wars of the Roses, which in 1460

Newbury's first, and
governing, charter – granted
by Queen Elizabeth in 1596

resulted in three commissioners visiting Newbury to seek out supporters of
the Duke of York, who were then either executed or relieved of their
possessions. When Edward IV, son of Richard Duke of York, came to the
throne Newbury was regarded as a royal 'appanage'. In 1483 the town was
the venue for an insurrection by the Duke of Buckingham's supporters in his
attempt to overthrow Richard III in favour of Henry Tudor, Earl of
Richmond. But Buckingham was later beheaded at Salisbury and two years
later Richard was killed at Bosworth, thus establishing the beginning of the
Tudor dynasty under Henry VII.

The manor of Newbury was now under the control of the Tudor monarchy.
Henry VIII granted Newbury to Anne Boleyn (his second wife) and then
Jane Seymour (his third wife), and Edward VI granted it to his sister
Elizabeth, later queen. It was in 1596 that Queen Elizabeth granted the first
charter to the borough, putting the government of the town under a mayor,
high steward, deputy steward or recorder, six aldermen and twenty-four
capital burgesses, helped by officers such as the town clerk. Bartholomew
Yate was the town's first mayor under the charter and the first high steward

was Sir John Wolley. In 1627 the town and the manor of Newbury were granted to the corporation and its successors by King Charles I. Upon the restoration, the municipal corporations ceased to exist until they had obtained new charters from the king, Charles II. So in 1664 Newbury surrendered its old charter, handed over the money, and in turn received its new charter. However, in 1685 it was *déjà vue*, as James II adopted the same tactics as his brother and again a new charter was obtained. When William III invaded England in 1688 at the request of political leaders here, James II fled to France and William III (son of William II of Orange) and his wife Mary II came jointly to the throne. A proclamation was made annulling the surrenders which had been made and the town's government reverted to the use of Queen Elizabeth's charter. Newbury District Council now holds the manor of Newbury.

In 1086 Greenham Manor was held by Henry de Ferrers, whose family is said to have given it to the Paynells shortly afterwards (*Victoria County History*). The manor was granted to the Knights Hospitallers in the late twelfth century and a preceptory established there before 1338. It was seized by Henry VIII upon his dissolution of the Hospitallers and the order was later revived by Queen Mary and so the manor of Greenham was restored. Later, the order was again dissolved, this time by Queen Elizabeth. At one stage, in the eighteenth century, it followed the same descent as Thatcham Manor.

According to the *Victoria County History*, Donnington was probably the manor of Deritone identified at the time of the Domesday Survey. At that time it was held by the king. It changed hands many times and in the fourteenth century had passed to Richard de Abberbury, who in the late 1380s founded Donnington Hospital on land there. Thomas Chaucer, thought to have been the son of Geoffrey Chaucer the poet, bought the manor in 1415. Again the manor passed through many hands. In the late 1530s Edward Fettiplace (former servant of the Duke of Suffolk) appears to have been steward of the manor. At the time of the seige of Donnington Castle, during the civil war of the seventeenth century, the manor seems to have been held, says the *Victoria County History*, by John Packer, clerk of the Privy Seal. Since then the manor has been held by several MPs, among others.

The manor of Speen was held from the king by Carlo during Edward the Confessor's reign in the early eleventh century. In 1079 the church of Speen was given to the Priory of Aufay in France by Bernard, son of Geoffrey de Neuf Marche. William Marshal, first Earl of Pembroke, held the manor in the early thirteeenth century. Many of the inheritors of the manor died childless, with the manor passing to brothers or sisters and their children. Heirs acquired other lands so that eventually several manors existed. The manor of Speenhamland was one of the other manors. The original manor, which by the early 1400s was called Church Speen, became attached to the manor of Donnington and in 1568 was sold to the Dolmans, lords of the manor of Shaw. For a couple of hundred years its history then followed the descent of the manor of Shaw. Part of the manor of Speen was given away in the thirteenth century and became known as Speen Basset or Wood Speen.

The high ground of Wash Common got its name during medieval times from the area of the Enborne river valley known as The Wash. It was considered the waste of the manor of Newbury since it was such poor land. On the death of Elizabeth I the manor was passed to James I, who granted it to his queen, Anne of Denmark. A petition was signed by Newbury inhabitants in 1626 asking that the corporation should be allowed to buy the manor, and thus in 1627 the last grant of the manor was made to the mayor and corporation of Newbury.

It was one of the lords of the manor of Newbury – Geoffrey, Count of Perche – who founded the Priory of St John the Baptist at Sandleford for Augustinian canons between 1193 and 1200. In 1440 Prior Simon Dam was removed from office for allegedly allowing the house to become ruinous and the priory never recovered, its estates and buildings being granted to St George's chapel, Windsor, on the death of the last canon in 1478. The priory was converted into a house and about 250 years later its occupant, widow Elizabeth Montagu, commissioned considerable work on the property, employing the services of Capability Brown to lay out the grounds and architect James Wyatt for other improvements. The large mansion, now St Gabriel's School, incorporates some of the old monastic buildings.

At the time of Edward the Confessor (1002–66) the manor of Shaw was held by Aluric, and in the Domesday Survey it belonged to Hugh, son of Baldric, sheriff of Yorkshire. The family of Columbers or De Columbariis owned it in the thirteenth century and it passed through many hands until in 1404, along with Shaw Mill, it became the property of St Mary's College, Winchester. In the early 1400s the warden and fellows also became sub-tenants of Colthrop, a manor in the same district as Shaw. At this time Shaw had four or five watermills – for corn, malting, tanning and fulling. The college held the manor until 1543 when the king, Henry VIII, bought it.

In the late 1550s Thomas Dolman, a Newbury clothier and son of William Dolman (manager to clothier John Winchcombe), acquired the manor and shortly afterwards began building the Elizabethan Shaw House, a task which was completed by his son, at a cost of about £10,000. It was built in the shape of the letter E, said to have been fashionable at the time. Thomas Dolman is reputed to have removed the village so that he could build his stately house. His son's retirement from trade – following the completion of the house – brought forth the saying from townspeople: 'Lord have mercy on us miserable sinners, Dolman has built a new house and turned away all his spinners.' In the Civil Wars the manor was held for the king. Royalty was sometimes entertained there – Charles II and his queen and the Duke of York in 1663 and Queen Anne in 1703. In 1721 the manor was bought by James, Duke of Chandos, who did not take possession of it until Lady Day 1728 because of a long and complicated legal wrangle. After the death of the duke's widow in 1751 it was sold to Joseph Andrews, a London merchant. At the same time he bought the manors of Speen and Colthrop for the sum of £27,122 10s. Upon the death of Mrs Andrews, an inventory was taken in 1822 of the 2,630 gallons of beer and ale at Shaw House. Various owners kept Shaw House as a private residence until the Second World War, when it was requisitioned for use by the army and after which Berkshire County Council bought it and turned it into a school. This now occupies modern buildings in the grounds, while Shaw House itself has been closed since 1985 because of its poor state of repair. On display in Newbury Museum is an iron chest, probably late sixteenth or seventeenth century, which came from Shaw House and was used to store documents. It is not known to which family it originally belonged.

In the Domesday survey the manor of Donnington was held by William Lovett. It passed through various hands and in 1817 was put up for sale by auction, with all its quit rents, courts and rights, at The Lamb Inn, Wallingford. A Chapel of Jesus was rebuilt at Donnington by Sir Richard Abberbury (lord of the manor of Donnington from 1353 to 1415) after 1365, and in 1376 he granted endowments to the Priory of the Crouched Friars in London. The present house of Donnington Priory was rebuilt from 1655 by the Cowslade family and is now used by estate agents and auctioneers Dreweatt Neate. Sir John Boys, who was besieged inside Donnington Castle during the Civil War until 1646, had ordered the destruction of the whole village for providing support to his enemies the Parliamentarians, and so the original priory disappeared.

Some of the mainstays of life in Newbury throughout the centuries began life in medieval times. The market was already established by 1204 and the fair of St Jude's, which was moved during the seventeenth century to Wash Common, was originally granted by St John in 1215, one of 3,300 charters granted in the thirteenth century for fairs and markets. In this way revenue was raised by grants for the Crown and landowners were allowed to receive market tolls. Queen Elizabeth's 1596 charter granted the borough the right to hold four fairs or marts every year – the first on 25 March, the Day of the Annunciation of Our Lord; the second on 24 June, the Day of the Nativity of St John the Baptist; the third on 24 August, the Day of St Bartholomew; and the fourth on 28 October, the Day of the Feast of St Simion and Jude. At one time Newbury is said to have had eight fairs, including a July cherry fair. There were also wool fairs. The St Bartholomew Fair survived well into the twentieth century, but the only surviving fair in the town now is that of the Michaelmas Mop – keeping alive one of the last links with old Newbury. The Michaelmas Hiring Fair, as it was then known, was established some time before 1752. The fair was originally held in the Market Place and the

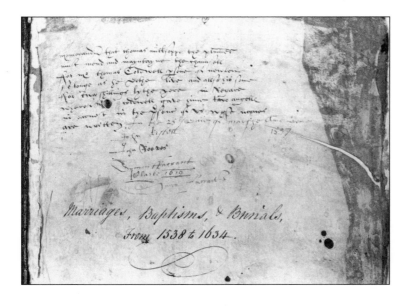

The earliest surviving parish register for Newbury, covering the period from 1538 to 1634

wharf, but was then displaced to Greenham Grounds in 1933 by increasing traffic, and by the early 1960s had moved to its present site in Northcroft.

The Black Death hit Newbury in 1348, reducing the population. The social revolution which followed it nationwide sparked off the break-up of the manorial system, and the functions of the local authorities such as the court leet (which in Newbury's case was presided over by the mayor) were gradually overtaken by increased activity of parliament. By Henry VII's reign, local landowners had already started to put themselves forward as candidates for election to a borough seat. Parish registers were unknown in England until the reign of Henry VIII and it is considered likely that the Newbury parish register was started to comply with a mandate issued by Thomas Cromwell, Lord Privy Seal, in 1538.

Newbury families begin to appear in the *Heraldic Visitation of Berkshire* of 1566, recently published by the Harleian Society. Heraldry, or armory, began in the twelfth century probably as a result of needing to identify important individuals when their faces were obscured by armour. The duty of regulating the design and wearing of armorial bearings was consolidated in 1485 in the College of Heralds, which began making visitations from 1529 to see if coats of arms were being used correctly and to examine new applications. Four visits were made to Berkshire: in 1532, 1566, 1623 and 1665–6. For Newbury the 1566 visitation includes mention of the Mansell family, for 1623 Dolman of Shaw, and for 1665–6 Barker, Mundy, Garrard and Ryder of Newbury, Dolman of Shaw, Hassall of Thatcham and Wynchcombe of Bucklebury.

CHAPTER FOUR

Mapping Out the Story of Cloth

Guilds were an important part of the medieval economy and social life. There were two sorts of guilds – those formed by merchants who bought and sold in the town and those formed by craftsmen who worked in the same trade. The Newbury Guild of Weavers was founded in the reign of Henry VIII and incorporated by Royal Charter in 1601 (the forty-fourth year of Queen Elizabeth I) under the management of two wardens, Cuthbert Godwyn and John Baynes, and four assistants appointed annually. It was granted the use of a Common Seal (effectively a stamp of authority). The object of such guilds was to ensure a high standard of craftsmanship by long apprenticeship. But although the Newbury Guild of Weavers was not started until the early 1500s, in fact the wool trade began in the town long before that. In 1206 part of the £1 6s. 8d. dues from a fulling mill at West Mills went to a monastery at Preaux, pointing to the cloth trade at this early date. There were also fulling mills at Bagnor and West Brook (fulling was the pressing and shrinking of cloth by water). However, by 1297 certain mills (normally the most valuable property in the town) were deemed to be 'ruinous and broken'. By the thirteenth century the weavers trade was established and in 1355 twelve Newbury clothiers paid aulnage of sixty-seven cloths. The size and quality of cloth were checked before export by a supervisor appointed by the king. Aulnage was the charge paid to him. A hiccough in the town's fortunes occurred around the time of the Black Death (mid- to late fourteenth century). Before that, England's main export used to be wool itself. Later, wool was instead made into cloth and mainly used at home – and so Newbury recovered.

Although it seems that the town may have suffered a decline in the late thirteenth and fourteenth centuries, rising fortunes gave birth to Newbury's heyday as a wool and cloth centre in the late fifteenth and sixteenth centuries when the two prominent clothing families were the Winchcombes and the Dolmans. At this time the town was of national importance and was associated with John Winchcombe, later known as 'Jack of Newbury'. Chief business centres of the town were the Market Place, the old wooden bridge over the Kennet (which had shops on it), and Northbrook Street.

Jack came to Newbury as a runaway lad from Winchcombe in Gloucestershire and was apprenticed to a rich cloth-maker. When his master died he married the wealthy young widow, Alice, in the Litten chapel in Newtown Road, which dates from the fifteenth century and was attached to the Hospital of St Bartholomew. It was the nearby area of Argyle Road,

The Litten chapel in Newtown Road, where 'Jack of Newbury' married wealthy widow Alice

Hampton Road and Derby Road which had the old name of 'The City'. According to Deloney, Jack was known as England's 'most considerable clothier' when he died in 1519. The cloth factory which he set up stretched from Northbrook Street right back to The Marsh, now Victoria Park. In his will John describes himself as John Smallwoode the elder, alias John Wynchcombe of the parish of St Nicholas in Newbury, and directs that he should be buried within the parish church next to his wife Alice. A monumental slab and brass in his memory were put up in the church. According to Thomas Fuller in his *The History of the Worthies of England* (published in 1662), John Winchcombe kept 160 looms in his house, each managed by a man and a boy. King Henry VIII and his first queen, Catherine of Aragon, feasted at Jack of Newbury's house in 1518.

Jack specialized in a cloth known as kerseys and sold his wares mainly at the Antwerp fairs. Berkshire wool was of high quality – so much so that in 1454 it was rated thirteenth out of forty-four kinds available. But a series of trade crises in the mid- to late sixteenth century at Antwerp, and other centres where the fairs were subsequently switched to, were the sign of less prosperous times to come for Newbury. Also the emphasis was shifting to cheaper and more easily tailored cloths from East Anglia. At this time John Winchcombe II, Jack of Newbury's son, became involved in politics and sat in parliament for Reading in 1553. Henry VIII granted the Bucklebury estates of Reading Abbey to John in 1540. He died in 1557 and his portrait now hangs in the council chamber. Thomas Dolman, the son of Jack of Newbury's manager William, had by this time himself become a wealthy clothier. He bought four manors, including the manor of Shaw, and in 1557 he bought Colthrop Mill. But he left the clothing business at the time of the Antwerp trade crises and instead began building Shaw House, later completed by his son John, and retired from the trade.

The seventeenth century was a period of activity for Newbury. In 1611 the Guild Hall (demolished in 1828) was erected in the middle of the Market

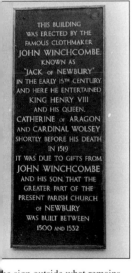

The sign outside what remains of the house of 'Jack of Newbury', in Northbrook Street

Place. In 1626 the Cloth Hall was built with money from the will of another wealthy clothier, John Kendrick. He left the corporation of Newbury £4,000 to buy a house and set the poor to work, laying down that they should be employed in trades of clothing. The building's first manager was Richard Derow, who was paid £2,307 3s. 9d. to buy implements and wools – including seventeen pairs of shears – for setting up the weaving shop and workshop. Work began immediately, for stocktaking took place in 1630.

But the seventeenth century saw the beginning of a decline from which the clothing industry never fully recovered. As an example, Colthrop Mill was converted to a cornmill and competition from other areas of the country was another nail in the coffin. By the beginning of the eighteenth century Newbury was making shalloons, a type of cloth for which the fulling process (and consequently the fulling mills) were not needed and in 1794 the Weavers Company, in a vain attempt to inject life back into the trade, issued an announcement removing many trade restrictions and inviting strangers to come and sell in the town. It was the woollen trade which made Newbury prosperous, but despite improved transport by road and canal the town could not compete with the industrial expansion of the north. Little of this trade survived into the twentieth century, although Daniel Defoe, writing in *A Tour Through England and Wales* in 1928, said that Newbury was an 'ancient cloathing town' which though little of that part remains to it, its people are generally employed in making shalloons, used mainly for the lining of men's clothes. The Weavers Company ceased to exist in 1905. Part of Jack's house still stands.

As the clothing industry faded, others took its place and the town survived. Government continued to develop and various national taxes were introduced. From 1662 to 1689 a hearth tax of two shillings was imposed and the returns give an indication of the size of houses at the time. Returns for Speenhamland show anything from one to sixteen hearths, with two or three being the most common. Other notable events during the seventeenth century included the fall of the ancient wooden Newbury Bridge, which had shops on it and spanned the Kennet, into the river in 1623. It was replaced by a new bridge which was swept away in the floods of 1726, when another wooden bridge was constructed. Building of the present bridge, a stone and brick structure, was started in 1769. During the winter of 1683 to 1684 a constant frost for many weeks is said to have frozen the Kennet river and caused floods when it thawed. Between 1740 and 1742 the Town Hall, or Mansion House, was erected. It was extended in 1878, but in 1908 it was demolished and rebuilt again, narrower, to make way for road widening. On display in Newbury Museum (housed in the old Cloth Hall) is a plant pot stand made from the oak of the old Town Hall.

It was at about the time of the late seventeenth century that maps began to make progress in leaps and bounds. There were few, if any, medieval maps of English towns. Roads were not shown on maps in the seventeenth century, apart from on plans of cities and towns which had by now made their appearance, and so John Ogilby's strip maps, published in 1675, were the first real aid to the traveller because the main roads of England and Wales were freshly surveyed using the statute mile of 1,760 yards instead of a variety of 'customary' miles. They were published to a scale of one inch to one mile and quite clearly show Thatcham, Newbury, Speen and Benham.

Opposite above: The earliest Ordnance Survey map made (one-inch) covering Newbury, 1817. *Below:* Plan of Newbury and Speenhamland, drawn *c.* 1970 by Brian Coghlan and based on the map by John Willis, 1768

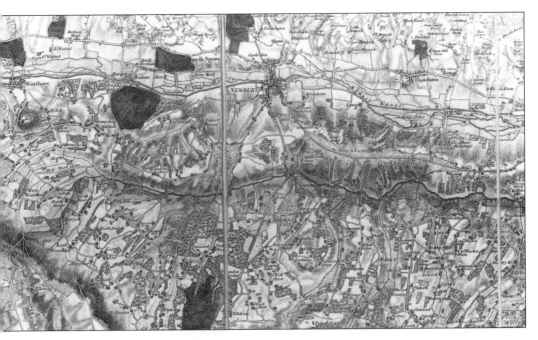

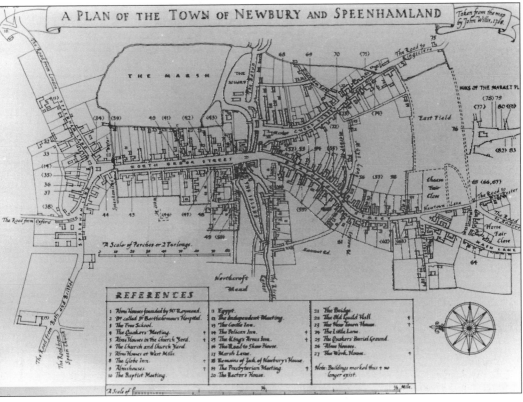

A PLAN OF THE TOWN OF NEWBURY AND SPEENHAMLAND
Taken from the map by John Willis, 1768.

REFERENCES

1   Alms Houses founded by Mr Raymond.
2   Dr called St Bartholomew's Hospital.
3   The Free School.
4   The Quakers Meeting.
5   Alms Houses in the Church Yard.
6   The Church and Church Yard.
7   Alms Houses at West Mills.
8   The Globe Inn.
9   Almshouses.
10 The Baptist Meeting.

11 Egypt.
12 The Independent Meeting.
13 The Castle Inn.
14 The Pelican Inn.
15 The King's Arms Inn.
16 The Road to Shaw House.
17 Marsh Lane.
18 Remains of Jack of Newbury's House.
19 The Presbyterian Meeting.
20 The Rector's House.

21 The Bridge.
22 The Old Guild Hall.
23 The New Town House.
24 The Little Lane.
25 The Quakers Burial Ground.
26 Alms Houses.
27 The Work House.

Note: Buildings marked thus + no longer exist.

Newbury Town Hall, also known as Mansion House, being demolished in 1908. It was rebuilt to a narrower width to make way for road widening

A 1756 printed map of Berkshire, surveyed by Emmanuel Bowel, has the county divided into its hundreds (an administrative division of a shire, which may have been established as early as the tenth century). It shows that both Newbury and Thatcham were in the Faircross Hundred, which also included Brightwalton in the north, Brimpton in the east and Welford in the west. The Ordnance Survey was founded in 1791 and its first one-inch map – of Kent – was published in 1801. Newbury was first included in an Ordnance Survey map (one inch) published in 1817. An 1849 printed map of 10 miles around Newbury, surveyed by Cornelius B. Davis, shows just how little Newbury and Thatcham were built up then. The almost universal tithe surveys of the 1840s are indispensable for property tracing and suburban development. Newbury's tithe maps were drawn up in 1842.

CHAPTER FIVE

An Englishman's Castle

L and usage and ownership sometimes proved a source of strife for Newbury inhabitants during the nineteenth century. Alongside the open field system which had existed since Saxon times was the common system, where farmers grazed their cattle on what was the lord of the manor's land but used in common. A change from these ancient methods of farming, which included common pasture, to a more modern system of land ownership, tenure and cultivation was achieved by enclosure but not without heartache in some cases. Often parliamentary enclosure was the final stage of the gradual modification, which had been going on for a century or more, of the common field system. Parliamentary enclosure was carried out throughout the country under the terms of private acts or the general acts of 1836 and 1845. The enclosure map sometimes merely confirmed an enclosure carried out previously by agreement among the owners. The enclosure awards registered the ownerships of hedges and other boundaries, and described the paths, roads, drains and watercourses. Charities frequently figured in the list of landowners on the awards in the Newbury area.

Most enclosures were carried out in the eighteenth and nineteenth centuries, but a few were done earlier than that. One example of enclosure was 108 acres at Speen Mead or Speen Moor, on the north of the River Kennet in the south of the parish of Speen, in 1738. Speen itself (excepting Bagnor) was enclosed in 1780. A preamble to the Speen award of 1780 shows that landowners did not attend a meeting at the George and Pelican Inn in July 1779 for fear of smallpox.

Another fairly early enclosure was that of 800 acres of open and common land at Thatcham in 1817, including Colthrop, Henwick, and Ham Marsh in Greenham. An example of a private agreement is that of Donnington as early as 1696, when agreement was made between the rector and nine other landowners and Thomas Dolman, whereby Dolman was to enclose 10 acres of land in Donnington Field, Shaw, in return for giving up all common rights belonging to Shaw Farm in Donnington Dene Field and other common fields in Donnington.

Enclosure effectively meant the fencing-off of a man's property and the extinguishing of common rights over it, but it sometimes meant the eviction of families which had settled in the area without having established a legal tenure. Enclosure was a frequent cause of riots throughout the country – and that included Newbury. When it was proposed that land at Newbury's East and West Fields be enclosed, trouble flared. A letter to the inhabitants of

Newbury signed 'R.F. Graham, your well-wisher and faithful servant', dated
30 September 1842, outlined the proposed enclosure and the disturbances of
a mob of several hundred which occurred the previous weekend. But in
1849 the enclosure went ahead and a 4-acre recreation ground off Andover
Road, now known as The City recreation ground, was granted to the
Newbury inhabitants.

Other enclosures went ahead without disturbances. What was described
as 251 acres, 2 rods and 23 perches of principally poor and gravelly, waste,
uncultivated and pastureland (part of the manor and borough of Newbury)
was enclosed at Wash Common in 1858. Papers relating to the enclosure
confirm that the nearest town or village greens were 16 acres at The Marsh,
20 acres at Northcroft Meadow, both with varying rights of pasturage, plus
4 acres of recreation ground allotted upon the enclosure of East and West
Fields. Just a few years earlier, in 1845, 261 acres of land were enclosed at
Greenham.

Land played an important part in another major change in the Newbury
area in the nineteenth century. The ancient system of tithes, which had
existed since before the end of the fourteenth century, underwent a major
reform nationwide. Tithes, which provide a detailed record of who owned
which lands, were established to provide funds for the church. Matters had
been complicated by the Reformation since many monastic holdings fell
into the hands of the Crown and then into lay hands. Originally tithes were
payable only in kind – the parish incumbent made tithing tours to collect the
tenth sheaf of corn etc. After a while money was frequently accepted
instead, but arrears often mounted. The case for tithe reform grew and in
1836 the Tithe Commutation Act was introduced. This meant that tithes
could be commuted to a rent-charge and commissioners, who divided the
country into almost 13,000 districts which in many cases was the parish,
were appointed to negotiate fair land values with those living there. By 1852
the commissioners had confirmed tithe apportionments which parcelled out
the rent-charge on land plots in most districts, effecting one of the major
redistributions of English property.

The 1842 tithe map of Newbury shows that the largest plot within the
West Fields, which at that stage was still unenclosed, was plot no. 96, a barn
and potato ground (arable) at 17 acres, 3 rods, 37 perches. The amount of
rent-charge payable to the rector was £9 6s. 7d. William Chatteris, the
squire of Sandleford Priory, owned plot no. 63, the largest in East Fields.
The rent-charge on these 42 acres, 1 rod, 3 perches was £13 19s. 10d. Land
in those days was valued in terms of what its rent-charge was, not what it
could be sold for, so the higher the rent-charge, effectively the more
valuable the piece of land. The valuer appointed for the parish of Newbury
was Cornelius Butler Davis of East Woodhay, who set the total rent-charge
for the parish at £363. Newbury's tithe map covered 1,722 acres, 0 rods,
31 perches, including The Marsh and Wash Common. Tithe rent-charges
were abolished by the Tithe Act in 1936.

Pasturage of cattle sometimes caused problems in the Newbury area.
Warnings were frequently served on people giving notice that their cattle
would be impounded if found pasturing on unauthorized land. One frequent
offender in such matters was William Preston of Winterbourne. On several
occasions during the 1840s a heifer of his was sold in Newbury's cattle

market to pay for expenses incurred on impounding the animal when it was illegally pastured.

The first British census took place in 1801 and has continued every ten years, with the sole exception of 1941. The census in 1801 showed that there were 1,242 people living in the town of Newbury, but by 1811 this had increased to 4,275. When the borough boundaries changed in 1878, incorporating part of Speen and Greenham, this seemed to have little effect on increasing the size of the population – in 1871 it was 6,161 and in 1881 it was 6,602. The last census, in 1991, showed that the whole of the Newbury district had 136,700 people living in it.

Commercial directories give a vivid picture of the commercial and social life of Newbury during the nineteenth century. Throughout this time agriculture was particularly important, as evidenced by the large number of farmers and corn merchants. The Pigot and Co. Directory of Berkshire, 1830, says that Newbury was the great corn mart of the county. The Kelly's Post Office Directory of Berkshire, 1847, says that the manufacture of wheat into flour and of barley into malt were the chief industries in the town, with the value of corn sold at Newbury far exceeding the amount sold at Reading in a one-year period in the early 1840s. At this stage Newbury had the largest market in the county. Other occupations frequently listed were beer retailers, maltsters and brewers – showing the importance of the brewing industry to the area – plus brick and tile makers, builders and carpenters. By this time the watchmaking industry was fading in Newbury, with just a few watchmakers left in the area. The Kelly's Directory of 1869 showed that one man, Henry Godwin, held no less than five public offices – including clerk to the commissioners of Income and Property Tax. Carriers were an important lifeline for provisions for the growing number of villagers around Newbury at this time and they were particularly prevalent on Thursdays, market day. The Newbury and Speenhamland Gas and Coke Company (for providing gas lighting) was based in Back Lane, Newbury, and by now the relatively new skill of photography had started to make an appearance in the directories.

It was in 1811 that the famous Newbury Coat was made, a great achievement which was challenged in 1991. The original Newbury Coat was made in 13 hours and 20 minutes – from a sheep's back to that of Sir John Throckmorton. The wool was woven by John Coxeter of Greenham Mills. Sir John consequently won a bet of 1,000 guineas that a coat could be made between dawn and dusk. The Throckmorton family is in possession of the original coat, but the replica – made in 1991 in 12 hours, 36 minutes and 26 seconds – is on show in Newbury Museum.

A grand get-together was held to celebrate the coronation of Queen Victoria. On 28 June 1838, 2,829 people dined together in the streets – Market Place, Northbrook Street and Bartholomew Street. The largest subscriber to the event was William Chatteris, the squire of Sandleford Priory, who gave £20. The tithing of Speenhamland held its own celebrations.

Other events of the nineteenth century included an epidemic of Scarlet Fever, which was to hit the town in 1872, and also one of Newbury's great social occasions was to see its last days in 1898. The mayor's Christmas breakfast of that year, given by Mayor E. Edmonds in the Town Hall, was

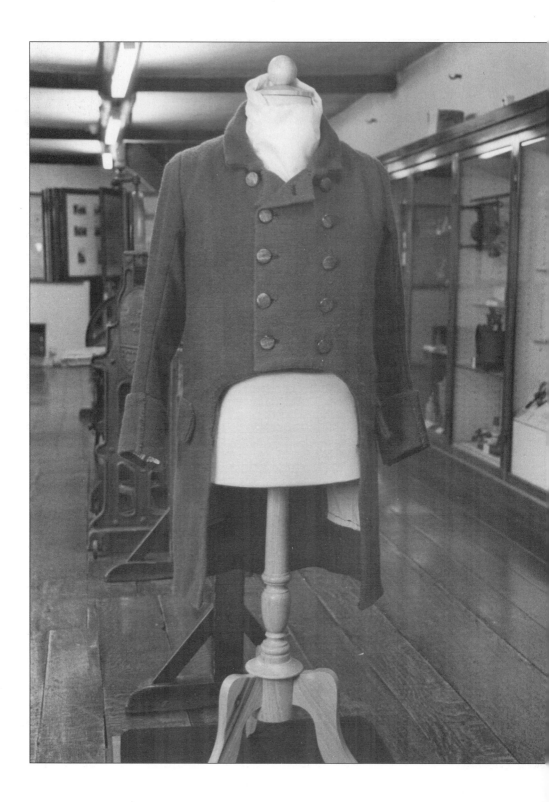

from wool to coat in 13 hours 20 min.,
on 25ᵗ June 1811 at Greenham Mills,
near Newbury.   W 8145.

ostcard depicting the making
f the original Newbury Coat
t Greenham Mills in 1811 –
om wool to coat in 13 hours,
) minutes

pposite: 1991 Newbury Coat,
ade at the Newbury and
oyal County of Berkshire
how in September 1991 by
raftspeople led by the Kennet
alley Guild of Weavers,
pinners and Dyers. The feat
ook 12 hours, 36 minutes and
5 seconds from shearing the
heep to completion of
iiloring. This was a successful
hallenge to the record set by
ie making of the original
ewbury Coat in 1811

the last of its kind. To take its place, future mayors entertained invited guests to sherry after the St Nicolas service.

Improvements in the lives of Newbury residents were on their way. A gasworks was erected in Kings Road at the end of the eighteenth century by an individual who sold out six months later to the Gas Company. Soon after, the corporation obtained powers to light the town under the Newbury and Speenhamland Improvement Act 1825. And so it was that the town was first lighted with gas on Thursday evening, 29 December 1825. The Act also empowered the corporation to make certain improvements relating to street paving, watching (the predecessor of the police force) etc. within the borough of Newbury and the hamlet of Speenhamland. Not all the improvements outlined in the Act were carried out, but commissioners were appointed to carry through many.

Local government as we know it today is a fairly recent development. Until the nineteenth century, the functions of local elected councils assuming responsibility for all public administration and welfare did not exist. Medieval and, in Newbury's case, Tudor incorporated boroughs had privileged groups of burgesses, aldermen or freemen who were not representative bodies responsible to the whole community, rather the incorporation of vested interests. The present local authorities were the result of the Municipal Corporations Act 1835, which created elected town councils, and of the Local Government Act 1888, which introduced county councils. Members of the old corporation in Newbury, who because of their office were trustees of the Municipal Charities, were replaced in this

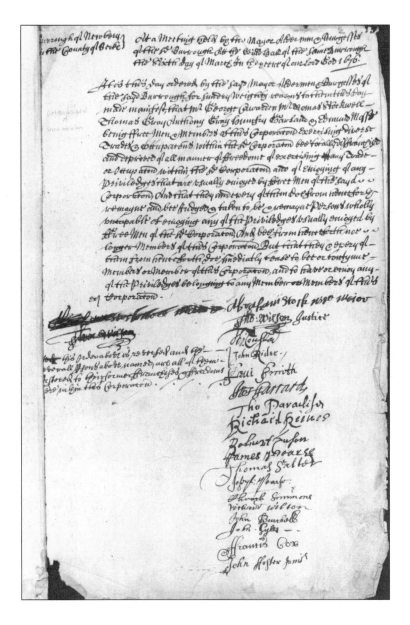

Minutes of one of the first meetings of the Unreformed Newbury Corporation

function by other trustees. Minutes of the Unreformed Newbury Corporation from 1673 to 1836 are kept in the Berkshire County Record Office, as are minutes of the Reformed Corporation from that year until 1974. The 1835 Act dictated that the town council should appoint a non-member of the town council as its town clerk. Robert Baker, made town clerk of Newbury in 1824, was reappointed after the Act. At this time the town clerk was the town's chief official, with the job of enforcing borough council decisions. With the 1835 Act, Newbury's burgess roll was increased and now included the whole body of adult male ratepayers of three years' standing. These

sie Kimber, who in 1932
came the town's first woman
ayor

burgesses had the job of electing the new town council which in turn would elect the aldermen and the mayor. The general government of the borough, including streetlighting, the police and the power to levy rates, became the new town council's responsibility. In 1878 adjoining parts of Speen and Greenham were added to the borough, which was then divided into the north ward (north of the Kennet and Avon Canal) and the south ward (south of the canal).

It was just six years after this that the then mayor, Councillor Robert Johnstone, attending a mayoring function in London, noticed that he was one of the few with no chain of office. He subsequently made an appeal for subscriptions for a mayoral chain, which resulted in a subscription list containing 116 names, from the working man to the lord steward of the borough. The chain was first seen by the public when the mayor wore it at the opening of the Newbury Arts and Industrial Exhibition on 15 September 1884.

Two years later Benjamin Smith, a corn merchant in Bartholomew Street, was mayor. On the occasion of Queen Victoria's Golden Jubilee in 1887, he gave a solid silver tea service, now in the museum's possession, to the town in commemoration of the event.

The town was to have its first woman mayor in 1932. She was Elsie Kimber, daughter of a grocer, and was the descendant of John Kimber who left considerable sums to charities. A memorial tablet to John Kimber, who died in 1793 in his eighty-fifth year, can be found in the Lady Chapel of St Nicolas church.

Several of Newbury's mayors have been granted the Freedom of the Borough over the years. The Freedom is a recognition of services to the borough. Before 1835 it meant that the citizen was able to claim exemption from tolls, but more latterly the title became an honorary one. It was given to John Rankin, who was mayor in 1899, 1900 and 1901 and who owned a drapery shop in Cheap Street. James Stradling, mayor in 1924 and a car salesman with a business in Northbrook Street just when cars were becoming popular, was also granted the Freedom. Frank Bazett, mayor in the war years of 1942, 1943 and 1944 and a partner in the firm of Pitman Bazett Solicitors, and Charles Adrian Hawker, mayor in 1912 and a photographer in Northbrook Street, were also deemed worthy of the honour. In 1969 it was granted to Maurice Paine, gents outfitter (now dead) and to Jack Hole, former owner of the Tudor Café.

Until 1948 the borough of Newbury only had an unofficial coat of arms, depicting Newbury Castle (really only a badge since it was not registered at the College of Arms). Copies varied so that there was no uniformity and the corporation decided that a coat of arms was needed to add to the status of the town and remind people of its history. The new coat of arms uses Newbury Castle as a crest, but also includes sheaves of corn symbolizing agriculture, a teazle representing the cloth industry, the wavy lines for the River Kennet and crossed swords for Newbury's involvement in the Civil War. The Latin motto 'Floruit Floreat' means: 'As it has flourished, so may it flourish'. At this stage the mayoral regalia was brought up to date.

Newbury district was created as a result of local government reorganization under the Local Government Act of 1972 and at that time the mayor took on more of a figurehead/ceremonial role since he ceased to have the power that he had previously. The town's charter trustees now care for the borough charter and insignia. Charter trustees are elected as councillors to wards which used to form the borough of Newbury. In those six wards they automatically become charter trustees as well as councillors. The district comprises the areas of the former Newbury borough, the rural districts of Bradfield, Hungerford, Newbury and part of the Wantage rural district, the rest of which has transferred to Oxfordshire. The old Town Hall houses the offices of the Newbury Spring Festival and occasional business is conducted in the old council chamber, although the bulk of council business is conducted at council offices built in Market Street in the mid-1980s.

CHAPTER SIX

The Church

R eligious faiths in Newbury are diverse – many have developed in response to the changing needs of the community as it has grown. Some have diminished, some have completely faded away and others have stood the test of time and even been revitalized, leaving the town with a mixture of old and new.

The town has both of the historic mainline denominations of Church of England and Roman Catholic – St Mary the Virgin at Speen is said to be one of Newbury's oldest churches. Both this and St Nicolas church in the town centre were Catholic until the Reformation, the sixteenth-century religious movement against abuses in the Roman Catholic Church. Now they are Church of England, the church created in 1534 under Henry VIII. Earliest historical documentary evidence of St Mary the Virgin church (and indeed the town) is in the *Ecclesiastical History of England and*

Mary The Virgin church, Speen, when it was being extended in 1859

Normandy, by Ordericus Vitalis, which says that the church, including part of the revenue of Newbury, was given to the Priory of Aufay (near Dieppe) in 1079. The church was rebuilt in flint in medieval times (1160) and a new church tower was built in 1734 – the necessary £159 60s. being raised by a voluntary parish rate.

One of St Mary's most famous vicars was Henry William Majendie, vicar from 1819 until his death in 1869. It was in 1871 that the tower was again rebuilt, this time in his memory. Majendie was instrumental in building St John's in Stockcross (1838–9) and St Mary's at Speenhamland (1829–31). The latter was declared redundant and demolished in 1976. He also carried out extensive rebuilding to St Mary the Virgin at Speen (1859–60) at his own expense (about £2,000). The latest alterations were made in the late 1980s by the then vicar, the Revd John Cartwright. In 1990, as part of these changes, the old pipe organ was replaced by a computer organ at a cost of £9,300.

The first mention of a church on the site of St Nicolas (Church of England) was in a grant of William the Conqueror to the newly founded Abbey of St Pierre de Preaux in Normandy in about 1086. Confirmed by a charter of King Henry II (*c.* 1187), the grant tells of 'the patronage of the Church of St Nicolas of Newbury' being given by Ernulf de Hesding to the abbey. Since it was not often that the grant of lands to an abbey were made when the church was actually founded and built, Ernulf is said to be the original founder towards the end of the eleventh century. John Winchcombe (later to be known as 'Jack of Newbury') provided much of the finance for the present church to be started, widely reputed to be in 1509 but now thought to be possibly as early as the end of the previous century (Bernard Eggleton, *St Nicolas Parish Magazine*). Jack of Newbury died in 1519 and in his will directed that he be buried in 'Our Lady's Chancel within the parish church of Newbury' beside his wife Alice. The church was completed by his son John thirteen years later. Sharing the honour of being buried at St Nicolas', according to the church's guidebook, are Bartholomew Yate, Newbury's first mayor (buried 1604), and John Kimber, founder of Kimber's Almshouses (1793).

One of the church's most noteworthy features is its Jacobean (1607) pulpit. It is thought that during the Civil War the pulpit was encased in plaster, but as the guidebook says: 'whether this was to protect it from damage by the Parliamentary troops quartered in the church during that period, or to hide the "abominated decoration" from the eyes of the devout, is not clear.' Several of the stained Victorian glass windows in St Nicolas parish church have been dedicated to leading lights in Newbury, including Henry William Majendie (referred to above), vicar of Speen for fifty years. Of special interest also is a window dedicated in 1884 in memory of John Smallwood, alias Winchcombe, 'to whose munificence the erection of the church is mainly due', and another to James Henry Godding, organist from 1865 to 1884.

One of the oldest bells in the country, dating back to the 1300s, is said to be housed at St Michael and All Angels (Enborne parish church).

Many of Newbury's mainline churches of today started out life in much smaller premises than the current buildings. St George The Martyr, at Wash Common, was preceded by a little brick-built church called St Luke's for fifty-seven years. At first it had been known as St John's Mission Room and Infant School, illustrating one of the many links between religion and

Opposite above: St Nicolas church from across the Kenne Photograph of a watercolour by G. Shepherd, 1819. *Below.* St Nicolas parish church toda*

education in the Newbury area. The first record of St John's Mission Room, an offshoot of St John's parish church in Newbury, comes from an article, which appeared in the *Newbury Weekly News* of December 1876, saying that a room had been erected on Wash Common in connection with St John's. The first stage of St George's church was completed in 1933 at a cost of £5,468. Dedicated to England's patron soldier-saint, St George, the church commemorates the fallen of the First World War and also the men who died in Newbury during the Civil War. In 1933, when St George's church came into use, the old church of St Luke became St George's Hall. A new hall was subsequently built in 1973, at a cost of £15,000, and the old St John's Mission Room was leased to the New Era Players, who use it as a small private theatre.

St Joseph's Roman Catholic church in London Road, Newbury, began life, according to a history of St Joseph's (produced in 1928), in a small and humble way in 1853 – one of the 1,100 churches built in the great church-building programme of the nineteenth century which took place to meet the needs of a rapidly growing population and the rise of urban areas. One of the priests of St Mary's College, Woolhampton, bought No. 105 London Road with the adjoining land and established the first mass centre. In 1864 a church – 'resembling more than anything else a country wayside chapel' – was built next to the presbytery at a cost of £800. This became the current church hall when the new church was opened in 1928 (building cost £15,000) to cope with an increasing congregation. According to the church history: 'The new church sets out on her mission under the most favourable auspices. The old bigotry and prejudice against the Catholic religion – born of ignorance – has practically died out, and Catholics and their non-Catholic fellow-townsmen live and work together in peace and Christian friendship.'

An English church census by Marc Europe of over 6,000 churches nationally analysed church-going between 1979 and 1989. Overall it showed that eight times more people attend church than go to league football matches each week. Within the area which includes Berkshire just under 340,000 adults or 8.4 per cent of the adult population were in church on Sunday 15 October 1989, compared with the national norm of 9.5 per cent.

The Roman Catholics had the largest adult congregations in Berkshire, with an average Sunday mass attendance of 192 per church, much lower than the national average of 341 for Catholics. In Newbury too, the Catholics seem to have larger congregations than many of the other churches. For example, at St Joseph's Father Vincent Harvey says that the total Sunday congregation ranges from 360 to 440, although in 1970 the average attending mass at the church was 506. This apparent decline obscures the fact that since then the congregations at Wash Common (St Francis De Sales, built 1968) and at Thatcham (Our Lady of the Assumption, built 1977) have both been developed.

The Marc Europe report, in its conclusions about the area including Berkshire, asks: 'How can churches become more welcoming and caring towards newcomers? How can church life be made more relevant to teenagers and young adults?'

The revitalization of St Mary's at Speen is perhaps indicative of every church's hopes for future growth. The Revd John Cartwright, at the church from 1985 to 1993, said: 'It was a broken-down church – there had been no heating for seven years. Every time it rained it flooded. The main service was in a school and we had an average of thirty people there.' He was given money by the diocese to repair the church and within six months services were being held there again. By 1993 there were about a hundred Sunday church-goers.

The Marc Europe report also asks: 'Will Christianity become increasingly irrelevant to large sections of society?' Perhaps, in the fast pace of today's world, the Revd Cartwight has the answer: 'The art of a good sermon is to get a good beginning, a good end and to get the two as close together as possible. If you can't say what you are going to say in five minutes, you may as well pack it in.'

Free churches (including Methodist, Baptist, United Reformed church, Independent, Pentecostal, The Seventh Day Adventists, Quakers and Salvation Army) have seen quite considerable growth between 1985 and 1989 (11 per cent) according to the English church census. Certainly many such churches within the Newbury and Thatcham area seem to be flourishing in the early '90s, but it has not been easily achieved. Declining numbers and sheer economics have left their mark on some churches in the area, with several groups having to close down small country chapels and merge with others nearby. For some of them, moving with the times seems to mean realizing that they simply cannot survive on their own and they would be better off combining with other groups.

The Christian Brethren in Newbury, which has met at its own purpose-built premises called the Kennet Gospel Hall in Kennet Road since 1935, is one of those suffering from a shrinking congregation. The present congregation says that their decline in numbers has been partly caused by a group of people leaving in the mid-1980s to start up a new independent church in Wash Common, called Glendale church.

Another Brethren group in Newbury – sometimes known as the Exclusive Brethren – says that its numbers are growing. Meeting in a new hall built by members in the mid-1970s to replace an older room which had been a seventeenth-century Baptist chapel, the congregation is said to be variable up to a hundred. Asked about the controversy over the Exclusive Brethren being accused of breaking up families, a spokesman said: 'We are not extreme as is often made out. We follow the scriptures as our guides and most of the things that have got into the press are not true. Our families probably stay together more than any other. All this about us breaking up families isn't true. We do only eat with those that we break bread with – in other words those that believe the same as we do.'

Methodism in the Newbury area has suffered greatly from lack of money over the years. In February 1990 a new suite of premises was opened next to the Northbrook Street church, celebrating 250 years of Methodism in the area and combining five churches (Bartholomew Street, The City Mission, Northbrook Street, Stroud Green and Wash Common). The movement started in Newbury in the first half of the eighteenth century, with its surrounding villages setting up their own small Methodist organizations. It was in 1740 that Methodist founder John Wesley, an ordained Anglican and controversial preacher, preached in St Nicolas church. But the Church of England closed its pulpits to the Methodists because of the 'rabblish' crowds who attended some of the meetings, and so Methodists found

The former Methodist church in Stroud Green, Newbury – now a private house

alternative premises – in Newbury in a chapel in Cheap Street. Rising numbers meant a new home was found in 1755 in rented buildings in Northbrook Street, near the present property. In 1804 their first purpose-built church was built on part of that land, which they had by then bought, and in 1837 a new chapel was built on land alongside, which the Northbrook Street congregation had bought for £850 from businessman Thomas Claxton.

But money troubles were already becoming evident and one of the minister's houses, in West Mills, was repossessed. At the same time agricultural wages were in many cases falling and putting stress on the small village chapels. In 1840 there were twenty-five Methodist congregations in the Newbury circuit (some in chapels, some in houses), but by 1891 only fifteen of these survived, being joined by several new churches. By the mid-1800s the Primitive Methodists, a group which started up in the early nineteenth century accusing the Wesleyan Methodists of abandoning the true Methodist spirit and fervour, had their own building in Bartholomew Street, a small circuit of village churches and plans for a new little chapel at Wash Common. Primitive Methodist churches were built in 1874 at Essex Street (Wash Common) and Stroud Green.

In the 1930s the Primitive Methodist church and the Wesleyan Methodist church (along with the United Methodist church unrepresented in Newbury) were united as the worldwide Methodist church, but true Methodist unity was not achieved immediately. Also, economic troubles were once again on their way. In 1942 part of the front wall of the Bartholomew Street church collapsed during morning service. After the war money shortages were made worse by the falling numbers, brought about by the impact of television and the fact that older members, who moved away or died, were not being replaced. At this stage the virginia creeper, which covered the walls of Northbrook Street church, was removed in order to save the

Day school of the Wesleyan Methodist church in Northbrook Street, opened in 1840. Originally the building had a first floor. The remainder was demolished in 1989

church's stonework from further damage. At the same time the churches at Bartholomew Street and Stroud Green formed close links and raised enough money to buy land off Andover Road.

In 1962 the Bartholomew Street chapel was declared unsafe and was demolished and in 1966 the congregations there and at Stroud Green effectively merged. The Methodist Buildings Committee in Manchester would not allow work to be started on the new site in Andover Road until money was available from the sale of the Stroud Green chapel, but by the time the sale had gone through (in 1971) the budgeted £20,000 was inadequate. By this time the two congregations were sharing Sunday services with Northbrook Street. Finally, after much toing and froing, the new suite of premises was built next to the Northbrook Street church and the Stroud Green hall was sold to the St John Ambulance Brigade and is now a private house. The Wash Common chapel was closed for worship in the early 1990s, sold and converted into a house.

Newbury's United Reformed church – formed in 1972 when the Congregational church joined forces with the Presbyterian church and later in 1981 a smaller sect called The Churches of Christ – has felt the pinch moneywise in its village chapels. But at the end of 1990 there was a heaven-sent gift which looks like providing some income for the main church. During renovations on the lecture hall (previously the old school room), an old tin trunk containing about 300 lantern slides dating from the late 1860s was found under the floor. Total refurbishment of the lecture hall is expected to cost over £120,000, to be finished in the mid-1990s.

Newbury's Congregational church worshippers got together from the 1660s in people's houses. According to the Lambeth Return of 1669 the number was normally at least 600. According to the *History of the Berkshire, South Oxon and South Bucks Congregational Churches*, by W.H. Summers (1905), in 1672 the Revd Benjamin Woodbridge was licensed as a Presbyterian teacher to hold services in Newbury Town Hall. A few days after the licence was issued, it was announced that public buildings could not be used for non-conformist services. It was in 1687 that a barn on the present church site in Cromwell Place started to be used as a meeting place of both the Presbyterian and Independent congregations. This continued until 1697 when, according to Summers, an argument took place and the Presbyterians built their own premises, called The Upper Meeting House, at Toomers Court. In 1716 the Independents re-built their barn premises.

All of this activity so far on the Cromwell Place site had occurred during the ministry of the Revd Benjamin Merriman, who succeeded the Revd Benjamin Woodbridge as minister of the Independents in 1686. The Revd John Southwell became pastor of the Presbyterians in 1688. Much re-building work has taken place since then – a new chapel, in 1822, is said to have cost £3,113 1s. 8d. – and the present church was built in 1962. Part of the URC's current financial security is due to the site's redevelopment in 1962 which was partly paid for by combining with commercial interests – there are now offices and car parking too.

The Newbury Congregational church had oversight of several village chapels which have fallen by the wayside – Ecchinswell, dating from 1860, is now a private house; East Woodhay, erected in 1804; Weston, built in 1831; and Hamstead Marshall, which cost £152 to build. All these have now closed, victims of dwindling congregations and lack of money. The only surviving village chapel from the Congregational church, now the URC, is at Wash Water. In 1947 a group broke away from the main Wash Water chapel, which was Methodist and had been erected in 1833, over plans to attract younger folk and had a Nissen hut erected near the old railway bridge. The original Wash Water chapel, which held its last service in 1975, is now a private house known as Chapel Cottage. The Nissen hut chapel, originally Congregational but now URC, still houses meetings but stands right in the path of Newbury's proposed western by-pass and the congregation will have to find a new home.

Baptists have also seen the number of their village chapels around Newbury whittled away so that there is now only one left – at Long Lane. Others, at Ashmore Green, Berries Bank, Headley and Newtown, are now closed for worship, but it was in 1985 that one of the half a dozen or so new Baptist churches to be started within Berkshire in the 1980s was opened in Wheelers' Green Way, Thatcham. The chapel at Ashmore Green was built in 1866 but was declared unsafe in 1961. In the early 1990s it was demolished and a replacement built, now a private dwelling in the style of the old chapel. Minister, the Revd Grenville Overton, said 'The reason for the closures by and large is because of the declining rural population together with the declining number of those with active faith.'

Newbury's Baptist church is one of the oldest in the country. The reason frequently given for the foundation of the church in the town in 1640 is that there were many Baptists within the ranks of Cromwell's army and that it was not surprising that the church should be set up because Newbury was such an important landmark in the English Civil War. But there seems to be no logical reason for this since Newbury's part in the Civil War would hardly have given the army time to attend church. The town's Baptist church recently celebrated its 350th anniversary at the same time as opening an extension and renewal of buildings, costing more than £300,000. Newbury Baptists had first met in the house of Thomas Merriman, who is commemorated by Thomas Merriman Court, a sheltered housing scheme in the town for the elderly. Other meeting places included a room above the present Camp Hopson's department store and a chapel in Northbrook Street, where Marks and Spencer store now stands. It was a deacon called Mr A.P. Morton who bought the land in Cheap Street where the church moved to in 1940 and is still there today.

In Newbury the Bible Pattern Pentecostal church was founded in 1933 as a result of a pioneer Revival and Healing campaign by the Revd Walter E. Smith and his team. Meetings were originally held in the Plaza Theatre, Newbury, and then the Temperance Hall, Northcroft Lane (now the arts centre) until 1962 when the church bought a site in Enborne Road. The original church on this site, now a church hall, was built in 1805 and was originally Church of England. A new church was built in 1979 and in 1991 a £100,000 extension of a hall and offices was added.

The Christian Science church, Salvation Army, Quakers and Jehovah's Witnesses are all sects included under the free church heading of 'other' in the English church census, a group which saw a 25 per cent increase in adult attenders in Berkshire between 1985 and 1989. A sect is a movement of religious protest, whose members reject the authority of orthodox religious leaders. Christianity itself started out as a Jewish sect. The Society of Friends (Quakers) – who have been represented in Newbury since the second half of the seventeenth century – are said to be perhaps England's only example of a fully developed reformist sect. Born of the Puritan movement, the Society of Friends was founded by George Fox (1624–91). It was in 1654 that the Friends brought their religion from the north to the south of England and during this period of growth Newbury Quakers were formed. Newbury was a strongly Puritan area and George Fox, on his way from Marlborough to Reading in October 1656, records that he 'came to Newbury where we had a large blessed meeting and several were convinced there'. The movement is said to have got its name from Justice Gervase Bennet at Derby in 1650 because, as George Fox recorded, 'we bid them tremble at the word of God'.

Newbury's most famous Quaker of the later half of the seventeenth century was Oliver Sansom of Boxford – 'Oliver's Cottage' still stands near Boxford church. He had several brushes with the law of the day, at one stage spending three months in the county gaol at Reading. In 1665 he had been threatened with prison by his adversary, Parson James Anderton, for non-payment of tithes. 'And further, for every Sunday henceforth that thou dost neglect to come to Church, thou shalt be as sure to pay Twelve Pence, as Thy Hat is on Thy Head.' Ex-communication followed 'for not Paying the Steeple-House Tax'. The Quakers' first meeting house in Newbury, off Bartholomew Street, opened in 1702, following the Toleration Act of 1689. This allowed non-conformists of every kind not only to have their own places of worship, but their own preachers and teachers too.

By 1715 Friends are said to have had probably the largest number of congregations of any dissenting community in England and Wales, 696 against the Presbyterians' 662, but the average size of meetings was smaller. From 1739 to 1748 Methodism was increasing and some Friends were converted. This is reflected in figures quoted in *Portrait in Grey, A Short History of the Quakers* by John Punsham (1984): in 1680 there were about 60,000 Quakers but by 1840 an unofficial census put the figure at 16,227. Quakers recognized the danger of not moving with the times and so, in 1859, it was decided that they would be allowed to marry non-members. Other relaxations followed, including optional rather than compulsory peculiarity of dress and speech. These measures were not enough, however, to stop the Society from dying out in Newbury at the turn of the century (Walter Money's *Popular History of Newbury*, 1905) and it was during the Second World War that meetings re-started – in the home of Walter Bentley, a borough councillor. Today Newbury Friends meet in a converted house in Highfield Avenue bought in the mid-1950s and extended in the 1990s.

Christian Science is another sect – but, says author Brian Wilson in *Religious Sects* (1970), a manipulationist one, which means that the community is not an end in itself. Mr Wilson says the manipulationists are people who have found a way of achieving salvation, which is mostly seen as the ability to attain such things as health, happiness and long life. The church was founded by Mary Baker Eddy (1821–1910) in Boston, Massachusetts, in 1879 and started in Newbury in 1919, with meetings being held in various places until The Litten property was acquired in 1929 and altered into suitable accommodation for the congregation, the total cost being £982. The church is known in Newbury as the First Church of Christ Scientist. Growing numbers meant that a new church was built on the site in 1959.

The date on a stone outside the hall of Newbury's branch of the Salvation Army (the name was adopted in 1878 by its national founder William Booth) in Northcroft Lane says 1883.

Numbers at the Thatcham Free Church fluctuate due to the mobile population of Thatcham itself. The church was founded in 1965 when the building, formerly a brethren meeting room, was bought by a group of Evangelical Christians as an independent Evangelical church.

Jehovah's Witnesses is an adventist movement in that its members expect the speedy second coming of Christ. Its Newbury branch began in the late 1930s and had many homes – including the Temperance Hall (a popular meeting place for church groups in the area) – until 1985, when it bought land in Pinchington Lane and put up Kingdom Hall (built for up to 250 people) for an all-inclusive price of £57,000.

CHAPTER SEVEN

Communication

A communication network is the lifeblood of any community, thus a good communication system to some extent dictates how a town develops. So it is with Newbury.

The marshy alluvium of the Kennet Valley narrows enough at Newbury for a crossing point which has served Newbury well since prehistoric times. Indeed, in an address at the Newbury District Field Club in 1938, historian Harold Peake took this one stage further and said that the street plan of the borough has its roots in the early Iron Age. He said that while sinking trenches for the town's sewerage system in 1895, workmen discovered in West Street a cheek-piece of a bridle made from part of the antler of a red deer, showing that travellers were crossing the valley by the Northbrook Street route before the Roman legions came through this country.

Drovers, people who drove their cattle and sheep along the old roads, were an integral part of the farming system which dates back to Norman times. Farmers in isolated communities in Wales and Scotland depended upon the drovers as a means of communication between themselves and the smallholders and centres in lowland England, where there was a ready market for their cattle and sheep. The drovers also acted as news-carriers when they returned home. Pre-existing routes, which had started as animal paths and been developed into man-made tracks by prehistoric man hunting wild animals, would probably have been followed by these drovers. One of the routes from the Welsh border passed through Avebury, Marlborough and Newbury, turned north through East Ilsley, where they joined droves using different routes from Wales. One of the oldest and most spectacular ancient hilltop tracks used by the drovers is the Berkshire Ridgeway. By the thirteenth century there were regular movements of cattle and sheep to a growing number of market centres, including one at East Ilsley in Berkshire.

Many roads were kept up by the abbeys, but after the Dissolution of the monasteries, they deteriorated. In the mid-sixteenth century people were required to give up a certain number of days of the year for road repairs, when in 1555 a system was established whereby roads were maintained by the parishes through which they passed. Under this system the labour, horses and carts and tools for the job had to be provided free by the parishioners. All householders and labourers, so long as they were not servants, had to turn up when requested to carry out road repairs.

One of Newbury's most noteworthy historic roads is the Bath Road (A4). Under Charles I the Royal Mail was extended to plebian use when, in 1635, chief postmaster Thomas Witherings established six new routes, one of which was Bristol to London. The Turnpike Acts of the early eighteenth century approved the setting up of trusts which, in return for a road's proper maintenance, were entitled to gate the road and charge tolls. Sheer volumes of traffic, including more drovers, led to the worsening condition of roads and the subsequent turnpiking of almost the entire length of the thirteen main routes from London by 1750, including the Western Road from London to Bath and Bristol. The turnpiking of this road was completed in 1743, with the section from Newbury to Marlborough (17 miles) being done in 1726. In 1784 Bristol businessman John Palmer set up a mail coach system with the approval of the Chancellor. The trial run was from Bristol to London. The Chequers in Newbury was where the mail coach horses were changed, a task done every 10 to 15 miles. The old mail coaches used to travel along the A4, which now takes a different route to that in the eighteenth century, in a privileged manner – they paid no tolls, the gates being opened in advance at the toot of the post-horn. The original run was completed in 16 hours, but when a mail coach was driven from Bristol to London by international horseman John Parker in 1986 on the bicentenary anniversary of the first trial run, it took 18 hours – this did, however, set a new record of 130 miles continuous driving.

An Act, dated 1770, for repairing the road from Speenhamland to Marlborough gave examples of tolls to be charged in the Marlborough district. These varied from a shilling for every coach, caravan, chariot etc. drawn by six horses or more to a penny for every horse or mule not drawing. The Act also said that the trustees had a responsibility for lighting 'any dangerous or narrow parts of roads' so long as no more than thirty lamps were set up in the Marlborough district and no more than fifteen in the Speenhamland district. Tenancy agreements for the Speenhamland district in the 1870s show that there were two tolls within that district – one at Thatcham Gate and Bar and one at Benham Gate. Another turnpike road went from Hursley, near Winchester, through Andover and Newbury to Chilton Pond. The hamlet of Halfway, near Kintbury, was named after an important point in the journey to Bath. And it was only in 1966 that, despite protests, the Halfway Tollhouse (several miles back from the present A4)

The former toll house, at the junction of Oxford Street and Bath Road, *c.* 1904

was demolished after its owners said that it was beyond repair. The Globe Inn, Newbury (where Lloyds Bank now stands) provided the platform for an annual auction for the right to collect tolls at this gate. By the late eighteenth century £130,000 a year was being collected in tolls nationally. Local trusts, which managed the tollhouses, consisted of dignitaries in the area.

Travellers on horse-drawn coach services often gave tips to the drivers, something which Thomas Cooper aimed to smash by paying his own coachmen higher rates when in 1827 he started his London to Bristol coach service, called 'Cooper's Old Company'. He also found a cottage at Thatcham, set up stables for his stud of horses and advertised for coaches to stop there, saying: 'You will find a good substantial supper of ham, beef, fowls, meat and pies, with waiters to carve and attend to you.' He went bankrupt in 1832.

A pre-arranged signal, such as a white card placed in a hedge or window, attracted the attention of the country carriers, who offered a two-way service taking goods, livestock and produce to market and returning with fulfilled orders. The horse-drawn service meant that a limited number of passengers could be taken. The carriers would also collect medicines for the sick and would collect and often distribute the local paper. The *Newbury Weekly News* was established in 1867 by J. Walter Blacket and Thomas W. Turner. At one time nearly 130 carriers were coming into town once or maybe twice a week. Speenhamland, near Newbury, was an important place for people to break the journey to the aristocratic spa resort of Bath and many inns were provided for the purpose. Horses were changed at the Pelican Inn.

Motor cars were first seen in the Newbury area soon after the 1896 Locomotive on Highways Act and the first motoring conviction locally was in 1898 when the Earl of Carnarvon was fined £5 for exceeding the speed limit of 12 m.p.h. down Wash Hill. The arrival of motor carriers' vans often

The Newbury Van, made by Plenty Ltd at the turn of the nineteenth/twentieth century

led to more passengers being carried and more frequent services, and some carriers developed their services to become true bus operators.

Both 1919 and 1932 were important milestones in the development of motorized road passenger transport in the Newbury area. In 1919 many men and vehicles were demobbed following the end of the First World War. Frequently they used their new-found driving and vehicle maintenance skills to provide themselves with a living. This, coupled with the mass production of the Model-T Ford, meant that many bus services were started all over the country. In 1932 Newbury and District Motor Services Ltd was set up, initially comprising three major local operators (Andrews, Denhams and Durnsfords). The company was formed partly to overcome some of the burdens placed on operators by the 1930 Road Traffic Act, but also to present a united front against the threat posed by larger bus companies who had become interested in the area following the Act. Over the years (before the outbreak of the Second World War) Newbury and District acquired many other local bus companies and coach concerns. In February 1925 the first all-year-round daily express service was started by Greyhound Motors of Bristol, with Bristol and London being the destinations, and the route following the Bath Road – the same as the first mail coach 141 years earlier, with Newbury representing an important staging post on the journey. Other companies quickly joined in and very soon new long-distance coach services were springing up left, right and centre.

Many changes have taken place in Newbury's road system this century in response to the colossal growth of motor transport. Back in 1959 the town's east–west relief road was completed, costing £126,000. Soon afterwards the north–south relief road was also built, both under the watchful eye of the Ministry of Transport and Civil Aviation. Together these roads were designed to ease the summer jams in Newbury town centre and to help the 15,000 vehicles a day (late 1950s figures) on their way. Long before the 1960s Berkshire County Council had lost overall responsibility for the A4 Bath Road and the A34 Newbury to Oxford road under the Trunk Roads Act of 1936, which reduced the county council to an agent of the MoT. The Berkshire section of the M4 was opened in 1971 and a 1989 government white paper called 'Roads for Prosperity' announced that 60 miles of the M4, between the M25 and Swindon (junction 15) would probably be widened. Survey work was carried out between junctions 12 (Reading) and 15 (Swindon east) in 1993 in advance of a precise plan being put forward. In April 1990 a controversial traffic lights system was introduced at the town's Robin Hood roundabout to try to reduce the accident rate there.

Water transport was much more efficient and cheaper for the transport of goods than roads, and by the eighteenth century London was a growing market for goods. Until then the River Kennet between Newbury and Reading was just a source of water and power for the many mills along its banks. But in the early 1700s there was a move to make the Kennet navigable for large boats from the middle of Reading to Newbury. However, the millers were against it (they feared the loss of water via locks to help the passage of boats would bypass mill weirs) and Reading traders did not want it because they stood to lose their advantage of being the port where goods from the west were laden and unladen. In 1718 John Hore of Newbury was made engineer and surveyor and subsequently reduced the long and winding water course between Reading and Newbury on the River Kennet to 18½ miles by cutting out many bends. He used just 7 miles of the river course – the remaining 11½ miles were canal. The Kennet navigation was completed from Reading to Newbury in 1723, after an extension of the original Act altered the deadline from 1 June 1721 to 1 June 1723. The navigation prospered and the wharf in Newbury became a bustling place, with goods being carried to and from Newbury and London. The navigation's success prompted its extension to the West Country, to link up with the Avon navigation which had been opened in 1727. The Kennet and Avon Canal Company was formed in 1794 – Charles Dundas, MP, was chairman and John Rennie was the engineer. Construction was started from the Newbury end in 1796 and the canal was built in sections. At Bath it joined the River Avon navigation to Bristol. Completion was in 1810. The original builders of the canal were known as navigators, or navvies for short.

The Kennet and Avon Canal (86½ miles long in total, with 104 locks), runs from High Bridge in Reading to Hanham Lock on the River Avon near Bristol. It took seven Acts of Parliament to bring it into being, the first being in 1794. There are three links in the chain of waterways called the Kennet and Avon Canal – the former River Avon Navigation, the River Kennet Navigation and the Kennet and Avon Canal itself.

But its heyday did not last. From here on, the canal's fortunes became tied up with that of the railway – each going in opposite directions. In 1852 the canal was sold by the Kennet and Avon Canal Company to the Great Western Railway. Standards declined, tolls were high and in 1877 the canal began to make a loss. In 1948 control of the canal passed into the hands of the British Transport Commission, under nationalization. It was in 1950 that Newbury man John Gould, who had set himself up just a year beforehand as a waterway carrier of paving stones, timber and top soil, with a pair of narrow boats, found himself cut off from the Thames when locks and bridges were padlocked for repairs and a stoppage notice was issued. Repairs were finally done but other bridges and locks fell into disrepair and in the mid-1950s the British Transport Commission announced its intention to close the canal. There was a public outcry and a 22,000 signature petition was taken to Westminster. The Act, as finally passed, relieved BTC of the obligation of maintaining the canal in a navigable condition up until 1963, but the right of navigation remained as far as it could be exercised. In 1958 a parliamentary committee reported that the Kennet and Avon was a good case for redevelopment, and in 1963 the newly formed British Waterways Board began steps to restore the canal with the help of the Kennet and Avon Canal Trust, formed to protect the canal from closure. It was finally reopened by the Queen on 8 August 1990.

The plant life of the canal has always been linked with the history of the canal. When the Great Western Railway Company began running down the maintenance of the waterway in order, it is believed, to eliminate competition between the two methods of transport, plant life was left free to flourish without interference because work on locks and dredging was much reduced and there was less traffic. In 1976 a detailed survey of the canal, carried out by the Newbury District Field Club, concluded that 'On balance, man's enjoyment and industrial development mean plant despoliation. . . . Canals are best left almost neglected as far as plants are concerned.'

With the coming of the railway, the canal's days for commercial use were numbered. Railways had three advantages: there were no frozen rivers, they were faster and there were no water shortages. For example, in the year ending 29 May 1841, £849 14s. 7d. was spent on ice-breaking on the Kennet and Avon Canal. In that year tonnage income was £51,173 19s. 5d. By the year ending 29 May 1847 tonnage income was down to £30,334 0s. 2d. A report in 1891 to the Board of Trade, as a result of complaints from traders and mill owners, said that in 1888 there was as little as 3 ft 2 in of water in places. It urged the Great Western Railway Company to dredge.

The campaign to build the Great Western Railway had started in Bristol in the early 1830s with merchants who were dissatisfied with goods transport to London (by road it was too expensive, by canal it was too weather-dependent and both were too time-consuming). The Great Western Railway Bill was passed by parliament in August 1835 and the GWR opened from London to Bristol on 30 June 1841. It was in the early 1840s that the idea of a railway to Newbury reached town and it had many enemies, among them the coach companies, innkeepers and barge owners. In the following few years there was much debate about which route the railway should take eastward from Newbury towards London: should it join the South Western Line in the town of Basingstoke or should it join the Great Western Line at the village of Pangbourne, west of Reading? In the end neither of these options went ahead. Instead a branch line, now called the Thames Line but then known as the Berks and Hants Railway, was built from Reading to Newbury and Hungerford by the Berks and Hants Railway Company. Building started in 1846, with hundreds of labourers being used, and the line apparently opened without public ceremony on 21 December 1847. This line, along with the Berks and Hants line from Reading to Basingstoke, had an original capital investment of £400,000. In 1832 an earlier scheme, called the Bristol and London Railway, would have run from London via Reading, Newbury, Hungerford and Bath – giving Newbury a home on the main line – but failed owing to lack of financial support. Long-distance commerce on the waterways was hard-hit by the railways, leaving mainly local traffic.

The Thames Line is still very much in service, but one which was axed under the cuts of the 1960s was a branch line which was started in the later nineteenth century from Newbury up the Lambourn Valley to Lambourn. The railway was the outcome of three schemes spanning twenty-five years: the first, in 1873, was a tramway system which was laid from Cheap Street to Donnington Square, but was abandoned because of financial difficulties; the second, in 1881, was a scheme for a light railway which would have had a junction with the Didcot, Newbury and Southampton Railway (then under construction), but this was rejected by the House of Lords because of opposition by Shaw inhabitants; the third, which received the Royal Assent on 2 August 1883, was a railway from the GWR main line west of Newbury. The first sod on this third and final scheme was turned by historian Walter Money, and following differences between the contractor and the Lambourn Valley Railway Company the work was finally finished by a new contractor and it was opened to the public on 4 April 1898. Just a few days later two boys were run down and killed by a train between Newbury and Speen. An inquest remarked that the line had laid derelict for so many years that it was used as a playground. The line was taken over on 1 July 1905 by GWR. In 1953 to 1954 a 3-mile branch line was built from Welford Park to an American air force depot. On 4 January 1960 the axe fell and the last passenger train ran on the Lambourn Valley Railway. Freight services were withdrawn beyond Welford Park, but carried on as far as Welford Park from July 1967 to November 1973, with the Ministries of Defence and Public Buildings and Works renting and maintaining the line from British Rail.

What had more significance was the Didcot, Newbury and Southampton Line. The idea was to link the manufacturing heart of the south Midlands with the port of Southampton, but it was perhaps too late and another route had already been established in 1856 via Reading and Basingstoke for through trains from Didcot to Southampton. Work started in August 1879 and just three years later, in April 1882, the formal opening of the Newbury to Didcot section took place. In 1885 the railway was extended to Winchester but never made it through to Southampton in its own right, although a bill had been passed in parliament in 1883. The railway was running out of money and in the same year (1883) the company's new chairman stopped the struggling company from going any further with the line. Through communication from Newbury to Southampton was eventually established in 1891, when a link was built from Winchester to Shawford to meet the main line from London to Southampton. The Didcot, Newbury and Southampton Railway was absorbed by the GWR under the Railways Act of 1921. The number of tickets issued at former DN&S stations, especially south of Newbury, plummeted when bus services were introduced as a result of increasing road competition in the late 1930s. A traffic survey in the early 1960s in preparation for what was known as the Beeching Report found the DN&S carried between 5,000 and 10,000 tons of freight per week (apparently three times as much as in any other peacetime year before). But passenger services were already on their way out and the line was considered redundant. The last passenger train between Newbury and Winchester ran on 5 March 1960, and between Didcot and Newbury on 8 September 1962. Goods traffic had stopped throughout by the end of 1964.

Many schemes proposed over the years would have given Newbury a link between its major neighbouring towns such as Swindon, Oxford, Winchester

Newbury railway station,
c. 1910

and Basingstoke. Most never got off the ground – only the DN&S provided effective links with Oxford and Winchester for less than eighty years.

Much has altered around Newbury with the changes (some would say advances) in communications: first the canal, then the railways and now more and more better roads. It was the railways which gradually finished the droving trade. Most of the cattle trade was taken over by the railways, but the Welsh sheep droves continued through the nineteenth century and in a lesser way into the earlier years of the present century. Within ten years of the opening of the main railways, nearly every turnpike trust was bankrupt. Commercial life on the canals was all but over.

CHAPTER EIGHT

A Poor Substitute

Links between education, charities, religion and health care in Newbury were forged centuries ago and still remain intertwined today. Nationally, schooling was inextricably tied up with the Church during the Middle Ages, but after the Dissolution there was no longer any money coming in for schools from the monasteries. Henvy VIII re-endowed cathedral schools with some of the monastic wealth and new schools were established in some of the six new bishopries, however not in the new Oxford diocese. More and more grammar schools were set up throughout the Tudor period, the reigns of Elizabeth and the first two Stuart kings. Separate 'English' schools also grew up after 1600.

Berkshire was said to be well supplied with public schools in pre-Reformation days. It had been thought for many years that Newbury Grammar School was founded by the will of Henry Wormestall on 2 March 1467. This was based on the work of A.F. Leach, who held that the Act suppressing chantries (passed in the first year of the reign of Edward VI, in other words, 1547) was executed according to a narrow and precise interpretation of that Act. From this Leach argued that only those schools which were part of the original foundation were 'continued' by the chantry commissioners, but this has since been criticized by other historians. More recent researches suggest that the grammar school actually started in 1547 under Edward VI. Historian Norman Fox, researching in the early 1980s, said that Wormestall's charity did not include teaching originally, and only when it was threatened that Henry VIII would take away the charity property as part of the Reformation did it acquire in 1547 an education function under Edward VI (as shown by the Reformation chantry returns). Mr Fox says that nowhere is there any reference in the chantry returns before that date to a school.

St Bartholomew's Hospital Charity is said to have become associated with the grammar school in Newbury at the Reformation, and was assigned a schoolroom and schoolmaster's house on the site. St Bartholomew's Hospital was effectively a town charity whose property, including the school, became controlled by the corporation shortly after the town was incorporated as a borough in 1596. The school's history during the early seventeenth century is sketchy since corporation records have disappeared. The school was closed from 1814 (when its master, the Revd Thomas Best, died) until 1849. Under the Municipal Corporations Act of 1835, the corporation was no longer school trustee and its management was passed to seventeen municipal charity trustees appointed by the Lord Chancellor on 12 January 1837. The school re-opened in August 1849 with twenty free boys and forty paying boys and it is now one of Newbury's few grant-

Thatcham's first school, set up in a dilapidated chantry chapel on the corner of Chapel Street and the A4. Today it is used as an antiques shop

maintained schools – the others are St John The Evangelist (C of E infant) and St Joseph Roman Catholic (primary).

Throughout the country there was a marked increase in the number of charity schools at the beginning of the eighteenth century, with an increasing number being financed by public subscription rather than by wealthy individuals. Where money was donated in wills for a school for poorer children, these were called 'endowed' schools. Thatcham's first school was financed as a gift from Lady Frances Winchcombe, widow of Sir Henry Winchcombe (great, great grandson of the legendary Jack of Newbury). The school was set up in the dilapidated chantry chapel on the corner of Chapel Street and the A4, which had fallen into disuse many years before. Lady Winchcombe had directed that the school should offer an education to thirty poor boys (no girls) from Thatcham, Bucklebury and Shefford. It was known as a bluecoat – or charity – school, where the scholar wears an almoner's blue coat. The school was opened in 1713 and continued as such until early in the twentieth century, after which it was used only in emergencies. The nearby Kennet School opened in 1957. The school, now an antiques shop, is a Grade One listed building owned by Newbury District Council.

It was in 1833 that the first government money was given to build schools. At this stage the money was given only to church organizations such as the National Society and the British and Foreign Bible Society. Newbury's British School (also known as Newbury Lancastrian School) would have been built with money given to one of these societies, as would Newbury National School (otherwise known as St Nicolas School), built in 1859 on open fields in Enborne Road, Newbury. Documents show that the school was insured under a fire policy in 1895 for £1,800 (premium £1 7s). There were a hundred boys and a hundred girls to start with, whose parents had to pay tuppence per week towards education. Now a Grade Two listed building, it was sold in the early 1990s as freehold premises with business use. The playground was sold with permission for housing. In 1993 the school was still in educational use by the owners, the Oxford Intensive School of English. A school called the National School of St Nicolas Infants was also established in West Street. St Mary's Boys and Girls School

The British School for girls in Railway Road, Newbury, 1890

in Speenhamland was also known as St Mary's National School. It was built in 1835 for the education of fifty boys and fifty girls, enlarged in 1880 and 1894, and originally endowed by the late Colonel Page. However, it was in 1813 that the first national school came into being in Newbury. Housed in buildings described as previously a storehouse and tenements in Northcroft Lane, it was leased from the corporation and run under Dr Bell's system until it was closed in 1849.

There were two national schools in Thatcham. The first one, opened in 1828, had been built using a £50 grant from the National Society. It was built in Broadway on the site of a delapidated almshouse which was demolished. The second – called St Mary's, at Clapper's Green on the east side of Park Lane – opened in 1846 and then the old national school in Broadway became an infants school only. In 1847 a British school was opened in Church Lane, Thatcham. It claimed the government grant and in 1874 became a public elementary school. A new council school (re-named Francis Baily School in 1964) was opened in 1913 at the eastern end of Thatcham, but by the mid-1950s had 545 on its roll instead of the 350 which it had been built for. Thus in 1957 the Kennet School, a new secondary school, was opened in Stoney Lane. St Mary's finally closed in 1964 and was demolished in 1980.

In 1847 state aid was extended to cover schools other than Church of England, with Wesleyans being included. In the early 1850s a Wesleyan day school was accordingly opened behind the Methodists' Northbrook Street church. It received three grants from the Board of Education for the year ending 31 January 1901 – an annual grant of £286 9s. 3d., a fee grant of £110 16s. 6d. and an aid grant of £59. Fees of £216 1s. 2d. were payable by scholars between the ages of three and fifteen. The school closed in 1908 with the advent of the new council schools.

By 1842 the Pigot and Co. Directory for Newbury shows that there were twenty-eight schools in the area, including charity, diocesan, boarding and day schools, and indeed by the turn of the century even the tiniest village near Newbury had its own school, often of the free elementary kind.

It was in the late 1800s that girls' education really took off in this country, having been pioneered by Dorothy Beale (Cheltenham Ladies College) and Frances Buss (North London Collegiate Girls' School). Indeed, in the 1883 Cosburn's Directory for Newbury there were six ladies' schools.

Charities frequently had educational roles back in the 1800s. In 1837 St Bartholomew's Hospital Charity became one of a group of charities which together formed the Newbury Municipal Charities. In 1848 it built a new school and master's house at The Litten, Newbury, but this school was used for less than forty years. Kendrick's Charity was founded by the will of John Kendrick, which among other bequests left money to the corporation of Newbury to establish a workhouse. The corporation received £4,000 to set the poor to work and in 1626 it bought land called The Castle (later known as The Hospital or Cloth Hall), on which it built the workhouse. In 1706 the corporation decided to use the rents of The Castle to set up a corporation (or bluecoat) school in Newbury. It was initially housed in the Cloth Hall but had moved by 1722 and conflict surrounds its whereabouts after that. In 1726 a new workhouse was built in St Mary's Hill, on the site of the current library, to replace the first workhouse. This was done because trustees felt they were in danger of forfeiting money from Kendrick's will as the cloth factory, also in the Cloth Hall, was failing. By 1831 a schoolroom also existed in the St Mary's Hill workhouse. Further charitable bequests were added to support the school, mainly by Richard Cowslade in 1715 and John Kimber in 1793.

In the early 1840s the trustees of Kendrick's, Cowslade's and Kimber's Charities also combined to rent a schoolroom in Northcroft Lane, probably in the previous national school building. Schoolboys were educated there until 1859 when they were moved to either the new national school in Enborne Road or the British school.

Another charity which provided education was Francis Coxedd's, founded under the will of Francis Coxedd, proved 1 December 1694. He left two houses at West Mills to be used as almshouses and other land in Newbury which would be used to pay for the upkeep and maintenance of the almshouses and inhabitants. Any money left was to be used to teach poor children in Newbury to read and write. A similar provision was made by Thomas Hunt's Charity, founded by the will of Thomas Hunt (dated 19 June 1727). He bequeathed a messuage at West Mills to be used as an almshouse by three widows, and £40 and lands and tenements in Greenham as an endowment. Once certain stipulations were met, any surplus funds were to be used to teach poor children in Newbury to read.

Children from Newbury can still benefit from a settlement made by Newburian John West in 1720, which said that income from his properties should go to help poor boys and girls in the parish of Newbury. The West Gifts Foundation allows such children to enjoy public school education at Christ's Hospital in Horsham, Sussex.

Minutes of the governing board of Newbury Union Workhouse show that in 1836 female children were already being taught in a chapel which had been adapted as a schoolroom.

From 1862 every headteacher had to keep a log book or diary (first-hand accounts of everyday life in schools), now kept mainly in the county archives. It was in such a log book for the Newbury Girls' British School that an inspector's report on 18 March 1874 was discussed. The entry said 'the general working is highly creditable. The only points calling for a word of criticism are the reading of the lower classes, which is not very bright, and the general needlework, which seems hardly yet to have reached full efficiency.' Log book entries for several schools show that absenteeism, particularly due to sickness, was frequently a problem in the nineteenth century.

Overcrowding was a complaint in schools back in the early 1900s, it seems, for an entry dated 1 April 1903 in the school records of St Mary's School, Speenhamland, said 'The school is dreadfully overcrowded today and we are very much in want of more desks.' Maintaining discipline also seems to have been a problem, with schools regularly resorting to caning as punishment. A St Nicolas C of E Girls' School punishment book from 1900 to 1925 showed that it was not unusual to find that two or three strokes of the cane had been given. An entry for 16 January 1911 in the log book of St Mary's School said 'Heard this morning that William Belcher had been locked up for stealing. Complaint also from Mrs Barlow that the same boy on Friday night after school threw a large stone and hit her boy, Arthur Barlow, on the head, rendering him semi-conscious. Belcher is a boy of the hooligan-type and a short time ago told the magistrates that the reason he did not go regularly to school was because I thrashed him so much.' An entry written in the margin, obviously at a later date, said 'Belcher was eventually arrested for a serious offence and sentenced to five years in a reformatory school.'

It was Forster's Education Act of 1870 which introduced compulsory full-time elementary education for all young children, saying that there must be a school wherever families lived, to be run by an elected committee called a school board. In 1880 school attendance to the age of ten was made compulsory. Kelly's Directory of 1899 shows an adequate provision of schools in Newbury, indicating that there was no need for a school board. In 1903 any school boards that did exist were replaced by local education authorities and as such county schools came into being. Board schools became council schools and new council schools were started. Lots of new public schools (private schools run by a board of governors, but not open to the general public) were opened, many of them as boarding schools. It was in 1903 that education became controlled by the Newbury Borough Council, whose first chairman of the education committee was Councillor John Rankin. Newbury's new council school started taking pupils from 5 April 1909, achieving the full complement of pupils by 13 April 1909. Both the boys' and girls' council schools in Station Road (opened by Sir William Anson MP in 1909) were destroyed by enemy action on 10 February 1943. Named after the education committee's first chairman, a school called the John Rankin County Primary School was opened in Newbury on 12 June 1956.

The Education Act of 1944 got rid of the term 'elementary' and introduced instead infant, primary and secondary to cover the different stages of schooling. It was on 1 April 1945 that Berkshire County Council assumed responsibility for education in the county and in 1946 a county primary school was set up in the form of Speenhamland County Primary School in what remained of the council schools building.

Opening of New Council Schools. 10.3.1909.

T. Fidler
B. Smith
R. Ravenor
C. Lucas
E. Gould
T. H. Pratt
F. C. Hopson
E. Harris
J. N. Day
J. Elliott
J. Rankin
A. Camp
Mase – C. Mordan
W. Edwards
J. [illegible]
J. Stradling
Mayor – T. W. Turner
W. R. Pettifer Gen. Sec.
C. A. Hawkin
Mace – F. R. Andrews
S. Knight
F. Garrett Lock Town Clerk
Rev. R. L. Majendie Rector
J. W. Righton Photographer

Walter Money, F.S.A. centre doorway

It was the Second World War which in a round about way brought Shaw House School into being. In May 1943 it became a school for boys and girls from the council schools when their own school was bombed. It was bought by Berkshire County Council in 1946 and that same year boys started to be transferred to Park House School in Andover Road, leaving Shaw House as Shaw House School for Girls. In 1975 it became a comprehensive school and in 1979 a co-educational school.

Apart from their role in education, charities have been responsible for improving the lives of many people in the Newbury area, and particularly during the sixteenth and seventeenth centuries money was often left for the relief of the poor of the town. Property was sometimes also left either to house the poor or to provide an income from rent for the charity's trustees to spend on poor relief. In fact, the town is distinguished for its almshouses, some of which have now been demolished. From medieval times poor people were cared for by religious houses, but with the suppression of the monasteries in 1535–6 the parishes – in Newbury's case this would have been St Nicolas – took over. In Elizabethan times poor law came about through necessity. The administration of poor relief was based largely upon the poor laws of 1597–8 and 1601. Under the act of 1597–8 a poor rate was raised from parish members for the support of the poor. It empowered the overseers (an office created in 1572) to erect a poorhouse from the poor rates, and work was to be provided for paupers. In fact Newbury's first workhouse was set up with money from the will of John Kendrick. Under the 1601 Act, parish churchwardens (along with other substantial property owners) were appointed overseers of the poor and those receiving relief were divided into three categories: able-bodied who were to be found work,

Opening of new council schools by Sir William Anson, MP, in Station Road, Newbury, on 10 March 1909. The schools were destroyed by enemy action on 10 February 1943 the impotent poor, and people who were unwilling to work. Vagrants could be committed to houses of correction.

The Speenhamland System of 1795, first adopted in the village near Newbury, became widespread in the agricultural counties of southern England. It meant that parishes attempted to supplement wages from poor rates on a sliding scale dictated by the price of bread. But it is said that it effectively encouraged employers to pay low wages, demoralized rural labourers and threw more people on to poor relief. The Poor Law Amendment Act 1834 became the basis for poor law administration when poor relief was at its height. It all but abolished 'outdoor' relief and made confinement in a workhouse the central part of the new system, making the workhouse regime as spartan and humiliating as possible as discouragement. Minutes of the governing board of Newbury Union Workhouse show 'that all mothers of bastards in the union workhouse be clad in a gown of linsey-

Dietary for Able-bodied Paupers.		Breakfast		Dinner				Supper	
		Bread	Gruel	Cooked Meat with Vegetables	Soup	Bread	Cheese	Bread	Cheese
		g	pint	g	pints	g	g	g	g
Sunday	Men	7	2	5	—	—	—	7	2
	Women	5	2	5	—	—	—	5	1½
Monday	Men	7	2	—	2	7	—	7	2
	Women	5	2	—	2	5	—	5	1½
Tuesday	Men	7	2	Bacon 4	—	—	—	7	2
	Women	5	2	4	—	—	—	5	1½
Wednesday	Men	7	2	—	2	7	—	7	2
	Women	5	2	—	2	5	—	5	1½
Thursday	Men	7	2	—	—	7	2	7	2
	Women	5	2	—	—	5	1½	5	1½
Friday	Men	7	2	Bacon 4	—	—	—	7	2
	Women	5	2	4	—	—	—	5	1½
Saturday	Men	7	2	—	2	7	—	7	2
	Women	5	2	—	2	5	—	5	1½

Old People of 60 years of age or upwards may have the weekly addition of one ounce of Tea, seven ounces of butter and eight ounces of sugar if requested by them, and more expedient by the Guardians.

Children under nine years of age to be dieted at discretion above nine to be allowed the same quantities as Women.

Sick to be dieted as directed by the Medical officer.

Approved specimen dietary from Newbury Workhouse, 1836

55

woolsey and an apron of coarse sheeting as for distinction in dress from the other females in the house.' Parishes were united into unions and Boards of Guardians were appointed at local level to manage poor relief in the parish.

It was in 1836 that the Poor Law Commission incorporated Newbury into a union area with seventeen other parishes, removing the care of the poor from the parish. Newbury was the head of the union, which included Thatcham, Greenham, Speen and Shaw-cum-Donnington. The Newbury Union Workhouse, known locally as the Union, was built in 1835 at a total charge of £4,900 on the poor rates. It was said to be almost self-supporting, the fields being worked by inmates or residents, with potatoes and cabbages being grown and pigs being kept. Police directed tramps for a night's rest to the workhouse. Specimen dietaries, dated 1835 to 1836, for Newbury Workhouse shows a pint of table beer a day to every man and woman. This was not approved by the Poor Law Commission office, which wrote on 17 June 1836 'The Commissioners have to state that they would not feel justified in giving their sanction to it in its present shape, it being considerably higher than the ordinary mode of living of the labouring classes of the neighbourhood and what they would be able to obtain by their own exertions. This objection applies principally to the allowance of meat, which on three days of the week is six ounces to each person, and to the large allowance of meat pudding on Sunday, which exceeds in quantity what the Commissioners have sanctioned in any other case. The allowance of beer as an article of workhouse diet is moreover contrary to the provisions of the Poor Law Amendment Act and cannot therefore be permitted.' The workhouse later became Sandleford Hospital.

In 1837 a group called Newbury Municipal Charities was established and consisted of St Bartholomew's Charity, St Mary's Charity (founded before the beginning of the seventeenth century to provide an almshouse for six poor Newbury women), Kendrick's Charity and Raymond's Charity (founded 1676 to provide twelve almshouses and a £600 endowment). Two

Upper Raymond Almshouses, built in 1796–7

more sets of almshouses were built by Raymond's Charity over the years. Accounts of one group of twelve almshouses built in 1796–7 show that 40,000 bricks were used at a cost of £1 8s. 6d. per thousand, resulting in a total cost of £1,288 8s. 8d.

Trustees were appointed to administer the Newbury Municipal Charities, but each individual charity managed its own income and day to day administration. One of the group's first trustees was Edward William Gray (1786–1860), a member of the long-established Gray family of Newbury. In 1883 Kendrick's Charity and St Bartholomew's Charity combined to form St Bartholomew's Hospital and Grammar School Foundation and as such ceased to be part of Newbury Municipal Charities. The remainder were consolidated in 1900 to form Newbury Consolidated Municipal Charities and since then many other charities have been added.

Another group of charities to get together was the Newbury Church and Almshouses Charities, formed in 1883. It included Henry Hobbes (founded 1625 for the distribution of bread to Newbury and Hungerford's poor) and John Childs (founded 1822, 1824 and 1832 to provide almshouses, a Sunday evening lecture at St Nicolas church and poor relief).

Almshouses provided a roof over the heads of the old and needy, but Newbury Consolidated Municipal Charities' records from 1900 to 1923 show that sometimes the occupants, who could be anything from labourers, wood carvers, bailiffs or drapers, lived barely more than a year after taking up residence. Often these houses were in poor condition and by today's modern standards provided sparce accommodation.

A report by A.J. Campbell-Cooper, architect and surveyor, on the structural and decorative condition of the almshouses of Newbury Municipal Charities and Newbury Consolidated Municipal Charities in 1931 said: 'The general state of the almshouse property is bad. That of St John's Almshouses being the worst and St Mary's Almshouses the best . . . The need of repairs is urgent. In their present state many of the almshouses would be condemned by a sanitary inspector, though they are by no means past being put in order.' In 1885, when the population of Newbury was just over 21,000, 589 paupers were helped (including indoor and outdoor relief), whereas in 1895 the figure had risen to 598. Gradually in the early part of the twentieth century indoor relief became increasingly uncommon. The National Insurance Act of 1911 began the provision of social insurance and in 1946 the modern framework of benefits was established. In 1929 the powers of the Guardians were transferred to local authorities and workhouses began to be converted into infirmaries.

Charities were effectively taking on the role of looking after some of the sick. A document, dated around 1900, entitled Duties of the Nurse (of Newbury Consolidated Municipal Charities) says 'That the Nurse's duties be to attend on the sick and infirm Inmates of the Almshouses belonging to the Charities.' As well as providing somewhere for the poor to live, workhouses were almost hospitals for the sick who had no one to nurse them, as evidenced by a workhouse standing order of 1836 for Newbury Union Workhouse, which had an infirmary attached.

The foundation date of St Bartholomew's Hospital is unknown, but it is clear it already existed in the reign of King John (1199–1216) – in 1215 John instructed Berkshire's sheriff to give all facilities to the hospital and to the brethren serving God there to have two days' annual fair at Newbury on the day after St Bartholomew's. Revenue from the hospital's lands was devoted to poor relief. At the Reformation the hospital seems to have taken on the role of an almshouse.

Nothing remains now of the Greenham Preceptory of Knights Hospitallers, which stood between the wharf and Mill Lane, and was established during the reign of Henry II (1154–89) and finally suppressed by Queen Elizabeth I.

A row of twelve almshouses, to be called Donnington Hospital, was founded by Sir Richard de Abberbury in the late 1380s when he gave 2 acres of land in Donnington for the erection of a hospital to provide homes for twelve poor men and their minister. He also gave the manor of Iffley in Oxfordshire so that the almshouses, which still exist today, and their inmates could be maintained. The de Abberburys were lords of the manor of Donnington at the end of the thirteenth century.

It was in 1930, after the powers of the Guardians were transferred to local authorities, that the Union Workhouse became a hospital and conditions are reported to have improved. The new Sandleford Hospital was taken over by Reading Hospital Management Committee in 1948 as part of the National Health Service. A unit has been opened for elderly, mentally infirm patients.

Another hospital which historical documents record is St Mary Magdalen, Newbury. Not much is known about it except that it was a leper hospital for women and that it existed in 1232.

The idea of Newbury District Hospital was born towards the end of the nineteenth century – in about 1884 – with the approaching completion of the building of the Didcot, Newbury and Southampton Railway. A nursing

St Bartholomew's Hospital, founded before 1215, is now almshouses

Donnington Hospital almshouses, founded by Sir Richard de Abberbury in the late 1380s. From Gray's *History and Antiquities of Newbury and its Environs,* 1839. Based on a drawing by John Osgood

ewbury District Hospital,
01

home had been set up in Enborn Terrace to treat the navvies injured while employed on the line, but with the building of the railway nearing its end it was clear that the Nurses' Home and Navvy Hospital would have to close too and a scheme was started to provide a general hospital for Newbury and district. Major Thurlow, of Shaw House, headed the subscribers' list with £1,000 and the site in Andover Road was bought, with the hospital (with a capacity of twelve beds) being opened by the major on 18 November 1885. The first patients were admitted on 22 December that year. In 1931 there was extensive rebuilding and renovation, with an enlargement scheme four years later which took the hospital to sixty-two beds.

CHAPTER NINE

Law and Disorder

P rimitive systems of controlling law and order have existed right back through the ages, but it was not until the Statute of Winchester 1285 – which reaffirmed a locality's obligation to keep its own law and order, and in towns introduced the watch and ward system – that there was any semblance of order. Similarly, the judicial system has not always had its present organized state.

Some of the oldest courts were the courts baron, a manorial court which enforced the customs of the manor and in practice dealt mainly with land issues, and the court leet, which usually meant a manorial court presided over by the lord or his representative but could also mean a hundred court, presided over by the hundred bailiff. These courts dealt with petty offences, such as common nuisances, and with the maintenance of highways and ditches. This system of manorial courts, which administered a local law based on custom, would have existed in medieval Newbury.

The court book of the manor of Newbury from 1640 to 1723 shows that the court leet was composed of all the owners of property (freeholders) in the town. They made the by-laws and their duties were mainly concerned with offences against these by-laws, thus signifying a form of communal self-government. In Newbury the court was presided over by the mayor. It was a strict rule that all male persons who owned property in the town should appear at the annual court leet. In the year 1641, no fewer than 348 people – the master and the wardens of the weavers among them – were fined tuppence, and a further 62 people – including many important Newbury men, for example Thomas Dolman, John Winchcombe, Gabriel Cox – were fined fourpence for not appearing. Fines included: 5 shillings for keeping a market on the Lord's Day, 10 shillings for allowing a cart to remain in the street, and even the overseers were fined 10 shillings for not mending the highway. An entry in the Newbury Manor court book records that the court leet and court baron met in the Hospital Chamber of the Cloth Hall in 1686.

One of the functions of the court leet was to set out the duties of the bellman, an important official of the seventeenth, eighteenth and nineteenth centuries in Newbury. Orders issued relating to the bellman in 1649 show that he was responsible for the better governing of the town from the dangers of fire and for the apprehension of all the pilfering rogues and suspicious persons. Most of the houses were wooden structures with thatched roofs and so careful watch was made against fires. There are many cases of inhabitants who were ordered to remove or heighten their chimneys. Other orders made by the court show that inhabitants evidently threw all their waste material into the ditch which ran along the west side of

Henry Beck, bellman in 1838, who was responsible for keeping watch over the town – an early form of policeman

Northbrook Street from north to south and into the Kennet. It was the bellman who opened the Court of Pie Powder at the town's St Bartholomew Fair (the Royal Charter for which was granted in 1215), held in Cheese Close (afterwards known as Fair Close). Its name came from the term *pieds poudres*, the court of the dusty feet, signifying traders from far afield. It was set up so that disputes arising between traders could be settled immediately.

Running alongside the manorial courts was the system of justices of the peace, whose origins were in the new land-tax imposed in 1193 by Henry II, although they were effectively instituted by Edward III in 1361 when the keepers of the peace became justices with power to hear cases as well as to bring them. The Act of 1361 provided that JPs should meet four times a year – hence the origin of quarter sessions. The JPs' (or magistrates') main function was the maintenance of the law. From the fourteenth century criminals were brought to trial at the quarterly meeting of the justices, although certain crimes were reserved for the assizes, held in county towns. Frequently cases were referred from the court leet and court baron to the quarter sessions.

The division between cases heard at quarter sessions and at assizes was blurred and only in 1842 was it laid down in precise terms. Generally speaking, quarter sessions could not try felonies such as theft, murder and treason. As the office of JP grew, by Tudor times the hundred courts ceased to possess much significance as a judicial force, although they were still important locally for land-holding issues. Shire courts, which had existed alongside hundred courts, declined in importance from the thirteenth century as quarter sessions became more important. Quarter sessions assizes were held in Reading, whereas borough quarter sessions were held in Newbury.

The office of coroner dates back to the late twelfth century and his duties include inquests and treasure trove. Until the Local Government Act of 1888 he was elected by the county's freeholders. Now he is appointed by the county council. Today inquests in Newbury are held in the court room in Mill Lane, but records show that an inquest, into the death of a new-born male child, was held on 12 June 1837 at the old workhouse. The jury decided that the child came to his death by person or persons unknown and recorded a verdict of wilful murder. The child, who died from a wound in the neck (severing a large blood vessel), was found down the privy of a house in East Fields, Newbury.

The oldest quarter sessions records in the country date from about 1540. The first recorder of Newbury (magistrate who presides over the court of quarter sessions) is said to have been appointed in 1640, although Newbury's earliest surviving quarter sessions records only go back to 1666. By that time procedure was well established. Offences which frequently show up in the Newbury records are having and selling weights and measures less than the standard, encroachment on common land and petty offences of theft. In the early eighteenth century the quarter sessions of Newbury were held in the Old Guildhall, built in 1611 and demolished in 1827. The last recorder of Newbury was Edward Terrell, who was appointed in 1935 and served until 1971. Quarter sessions were replaced by Crown Courts in January 1972. At this stage there were two locations for the

Crown Court – one in Reading and one in Newbury. Newbury's Crown Court continued to sit in the court building in Mill Lane until 1985, when this particular Crown Court ceased to exist. There is just one Crown Court now – in Reading.

Petty sessions were so called to distinguish them from the quarter sessions. There were usually one, two or three magistrates sitting locally, dealing with more minor cases. The term magistrates' court is relatively new and was introduced to deal with stipendiary (paid) magistrates in London in the eighteenth century, although it may have been in common parlance before that. At the beginning of the eighteenth century, Berkshire was divided into eight petty sessional divisions, together with quarter sessions. The Newbury petty sessional bench sat in the nineteenth century at 12 noon in the Pelican Inn, moving at the end of the century to the new Mansion House. Today it is unlawful to sit in licensed premises. Well-known names such as Rankin and Baxendale sat on the magistrates' bench in the early 1900s to 1930s. The advent of the motor car had a grave effect on the effectiveness of courts held at the Mansion House. The noise of traffic, along with the hustle and bustle on market days, made Thursday courts a trying experience.

It was the Municipal Corporations Act of 1835 which enabled over a hundred boroughs to hold their own borough sessions. But in 1974 Newbury's petty sessional bench was amalgamated with the Newbury borough bench, which also sat in Mansion House. The borough was granted its charter in 1596 and flourished for 378 years, but although many regretted its passing, it was also acknowledged that the public is better served by the amalgamation of the two groups of magistrates into one petty sessional division of Newbury. Now the magistrates' court at Newbury serves west Berkshire. At the time of the dissolution of these separate groups of borough and county magistrates, the clerk to the justices of both Newbury borough and Newbury county was Len Parmenter, who received the OBE in 1977. He once said: 'A court clerk is the stage manager of the greatest theatre in the world. In the courts there is comedy, tragedy, pathos and great human drama.' Before 1972, magistrates' courts passed more serious crimes to the quarter sessions. After 1972, they passed them to the Crown Courts.

A community's means of enforcing its laws has changed dramatically over the years. The Statute of Winchester 1285 rationalized the system of policing and in towns introduced the system called watch and ward (watch referred to the night duties of constables and ward was the term for their daytime duties). So it was around the end of the thirteenth century that the forebears of Newbury's own police force was born, under the wing of the town's watch committee. Newbury's police are first mentioned in papers relating to the seventeenth century; then in 1773 documents show there was authority for reimbursing constables for duties including apprehending felons and conveying them to gaol and watch and ward. An 1835 report upon boundary changes in the Newbury area said that under the local Act for lighting, watching, paving and improving the town, a police rate of two shillings in the pound for lighting and watching and another two shillings and sixpence for paving and other purposes was authorized on an assessment of one-third of the property value. Newbury borough police force was created in 1836; its first chief constable was Alfred Milsom.

The problem with watch and ward was that watch committees only empowered law enforcement in their own patch, not neighbouring areas, and it was early in the nineteenth century that this need for a centrally controlled police force was recognized by Sir Robert Peel, a British Tory statesman. At the beginning of 1856 the Berkshire Constabulary was born as a result of the County and Borough Police Act of that year, although the proposal had met with opposition, in the shape of a 532-name petition, when it was laid on the table at the court of quarter sessions on 20 November 1855. Newbury's first superintendent in the Berkshire Constabulary was Superintendent George Dowde and there were constables at Thatcham and Newbury, as well as surrounding villages. For the county force's first eight months (from 1 April to 30 November) within the Newbury division – it had a population of 24,939 – 113 prisoners were arrested and there were 49 felonies.

It was in 1819 that the Newbury Association for the Apprehension and Prosecution of Thieves and Felons was established to defray the expenses involved in apprehending and prosecuting people committing offences against property in Newbury, Speen and the surrounding area. Admission was one guinea for each parish in which a person's property lay, and the association, which was dissolved in 1888, would offer rewards on the apprehension or conviction of offenders.

In the latter half of the nineteenth century supervision of tramps caused considerable extra work and it was considered that half of the then current crime was committed by these people.

In 1866 a mounted branch was formed within the county, with one police constable at Newbury, and in 1894 the Bicycle Corps was formed, with one of the scheme's trial runs being conducted from Sandhurst to Newbury, some 30 miles. The eleven bicycles, which were subsequently bought, lasted until 1904 when new ones were issued to stations including Newbury. In 1915 Newbury had its first police car, a second-hand 15 h.p. Darracq, bought for £100. Berkshire Constabulary orders for 1938 show that the Newbury force did not as yet have its own police dogs. If tracker dogs were required, the then chief constable, H. Legg, said his men would have to acquire them from the 'Of Ware' Kennels in Wash Water.

Authorization for women to be admitted to the county police force was finally given in 1945. Newbury's first policewoman was Miss Edith Butler.

It was in 1875 that the borough and county forces merged and became the Thames Valley Constabulary. The force is now called the Thames Valley Police. In 1991 further reorganization meant that Newbury changed status from a divisional headquarters to one of four stations within the Newbury police area – the others are Hungerford, Wantage and Thatcham.

In 1992 the Newbury area had 155 officers, between the four stations – that is 130 for Newbury, Thatcham and Hungerford, minus Wantage.

Back in 1987/88 these same three stations had 110 officers. Over that same period of time the number of offences within the Newbury area went up from 1,239 to 2,159, although in the last three months of 1992 there was a declining crime rate. The national average for the number of police is 2.1 police officers per 1,000 of the population, but Thames Valley has one of the lowest police:public ratios in the country, with just 1.522. Thames Valley, which overall in early 1993 had 3,812 police officers, was allowed an extra 55 police in 1993/94 to fulfil its VIP duties.

The regular police force in Newbury has, over the years, been supplemented by volunteers. In 1911 the chief constable ordered a census to be taken of all loyal citizens who were willing to serve should an emergency arise. In all, 80 people in the Newbury borough and 148 in the Newbury county district came forward to be enrolled into the second police reserve, or specials as they are known today. Today specials are taking a more active role in police work, instead of background tasks.

Another change in the early 1990s has been the rapid growth of Neighbourhood Watch schemes. They are said by the police to be the fastest-growing crime prevention initiative in the Newbury area. At the beginning of 1993 there were 287 in Hungerford, Newbury and Thatcham.

One of Newbury police force's biggest incidents in recent years was on 19 August 1987 when the Hungerford Massacre took place, during which gunman Michael Ryan shot sixteen people plus himself. Two of the dead were PC Roger Brereton, 41, of Newbury, and Newbury's magistrates' clerk Ian Playle, 34.

Newbury's first police station was converted from two old cottages in Pelican Lane at an unknown date, although it certainly existed as a police station by 1878. It is now used by Newbury Community Mental Health Services. The station moved to its present site in Mill Lane in 1966. Thatcham police station was built in 1904 and is still used for the same purpose.

Offences and their punishments have changed dramatically over the years. Until the end of the eighteenth century, death was the punishment for all serious crimes. It was during the religious persecution in the reign of Queen Mary that the three Newbury Martyrs were tried in the parish church

An old print depicting the Newbury Martyrs, who were tried at Newbury parish church in 1556 and subsequently executed by burning at the stake

for heresy, condemned, and then endured the horribly lingering torture of death by burning at the stake in 1556 at the Sandpits, near Enborne Road. The sixteenth century was, ecclesiastically, a period of unrest and change. Newbury is understood to have favourably received the Reformation doctrines early in their evolution. The Newbury Martyrs were Julins Palmer, a schoolmaster at Reading Grammar School, who had originally been a zealous Catholic bitterly opposed to the reformed religion but who some years later began to see the Reformation light; Thomas Askew, of which little is known; and John Gwin, a weaver from Spitalfields in London, all unconnected. They were tried on the same day in the parish church in front of more than three hundred people, part of the court being John Winchcombe Esq., probably Jack of Newbury's son.

The executions register of Reading Prison for 1742 to 1846 shows that throughout the eighteenth and nineteenth centuries, highway robbery was an offence which was punishable by death. On 18 March 1820, on the highway near Thatcham, George Wiggins, aged twenty-two, was executed for robbing James Leach of The Angel, Woolhampton, of £15, a silver watch and other articles, and beating him. Another man was transported for seven years at Newbury quarter sessions for stealing poultry from a man in Speenhamland.

There were, of course, other corporal punishments, plus fines and exposure in the stocks. The Globe Inn (demolished in the late 1860s), from its position in Market Place, Newbury, must have witnessed the now obsolete punishments of the medieval system such as the stocks, pillory and ducking stool. The ducking stool, which appears to have been at the back of the Globe, apparently has only one recorded case in the borough books. Newbury District Field Club transactions of 1870 to 1871 give the incident as: 'that of one Martha Adams, having been so disgracefully punished, for the too free use of her tongue'. An Act of 1495 ordered that vagabonds found in towns should be put in the stocks and then expelled. The parish stocks also stood in the Market Place and for a while were stowed away in

...bury Market Place as
...vn by Thomas Rowlandson
...56–1827). The Guildhall, in
...centre of the picture with
...tocks, was demolished in
...7

the Town Hall cellars. They were used for the last time in 1872, when Mark Tuck was sentenced to 4 hours in the stocks for insobriety and creating a disturbance in the parish church.

Prison was a place where the accused was held until his case came to court, and it was only relatively recently that the penalty of imprisonment was accepted as a way of dealing with offenders. The Elizabethan Poor Laws, which allowed the setting up of houses of correction to correct the habits of able-bodied vagrants and to provide work for the unemployed, were where the concept of prison as a place of punishment and correction originated and it was during the eighteenth century that the boundaries of the common gaol and the house of correction became blurred. Reading's gaol, which sometimes took prisoners from Newbury, stood in Castle Street.

Newbury had its own gaol from 1684 when a prison was built on the east side of the Guildhall, which had been erected in the Market Place in 1611. Part of the workhouse in St Mary's Hill, Newbury, was also converted into a gaol at some stage. The Guildhall was demolished in 1827, the library stands on the site of the old workhouse and Newbury no longer has its own gaol.

Judicial records of the borough show that it was in October 1847 that the mayor of Newbury, Edward L. Farrow, received a letter from the governor of Reading gaol saying a charge of £6 would be made per year for each cell occupied by Newbury prisoners. The treasurer of Newbury borough objected to paying for the rent of cells, but the governor of Reading gaol said he could only accept prisoners upon the terms laid out by Reading Town Council. The bill for the year was £114 13s. 5¼d.

Religion was again the cause of trouble in 1664 when riots took place over the election of a churchwarden led by a Presbyterian, William Milton. But serious riots have taken place several times in the history of Newbury. It was on 16 July 1795 that men working on the navigation in Newbury rioted. And in September 1842 Newbury's East Fields was the location of rioting over enclosures of both East and West Fields.

Another notable law-breaking event in the town was an armed robbery at the Old Bank in 1815.

Newbury was where, in 1909, one of the national organizers of the suffragette movement, Miss Anna Munro, held her first meeting in Berkshire. She later became a JP for the county.

In the 1950s long lists of motoring offences made their appearance in court lists. The war years had meant a variation in the usual pattern of cases, with the theft of petrol and food as well as absences without leave being common. A serious offence was, of course, 'permitting an obscured light'.

Youth custody, a relatively modern sentence, was imposed in the mid-1980s on two London schoolboys, aged fifteen, for stealing the town's mayoral pendant.

Greenham Common air base was said to be an enormous drain on the resources of the police during the 1980s. B52s had been stationed there from 1951 to 1954, but it was on 14 November 1983 that Cruise missiles, a long-range nuclear missile first developed during the Second World War, were sited at the base. The peace movement became active at the base in 1979–80. Demonstrations and other activities by the peace women, who became resident there, and road closures when the Cruise missiles were

men protesting at
enham Common air base in
5

taken out on exercise, sometimes meant that Thames Valley police had to involve police from other counties, e.g. Wiltshire, Somerset and Avon, Hampshire, Sussex, Metropolitan, Luton and Bedfordshire. The Home Office helped pay via a grant. A group called RAGE – Ratepayers Against Greenham Encampments – was set up in response to the Greenham peace women.

Greenham Common air base raised two quite separate issues. One was nuclear deterrents and what the peace women describe as the simple issue of continuation of life on earth. The other was the extinction of commoners' rights. Commons Again was a group which arose as a result of that threat to commoners' rights. Supporters of the cause claim that in 1960 Newbury Borough Council illegally sold Greenham Common to the Air Ministry. They say that a council cannot sell a common without an Act of Parliament, unless exchange land is provided, and argues that in this case the public still has a right of access over the Common. But in 1985 the Ministry of Defence created by-laws to prevent people stepping foot inside the base and, as a result, in 1987 two women were prosecuted for trespass. However, the House of Lords decided that the by-laws were illegal. The following year the MOD announced its decision to extinguish the commoners' rights by buying them. Many of the commoners took the offer, but a handful said no. In 1993 a couple were still holding out.

Peace woman Evelyn Parker says that court cases brought by Commons Again have failed to prove that the extinction of the rights is illegal and the MOD cannot prove it has extinguished the rights, since not all the commoners have accepted the offer. So, despite the fact that the Cruise missiles were withdrawn from the base in the summer of 1991 and the Americans left the base on 11 September 1992, still the question mark hangs over the future of Greenham Common. The Americans have left many facilities behind at the base – housing and leisure facilities, for example. Although Commons Again wants the base to return to open space, peace woman Evelyn Parker says they realize it is unrealistic to expect these buildings to be knocked down. Various proposals have been put forward for the base's use, but nothing has been resolved. In March 1992 the Ministry of Defence said that much of Greenham Common would be returned to open space when it is no longer needed for military use. In autumn 1993 Newbury District Council had four planning applications for the disused airfield: 1, to use the hangars for a film studio; 2, to dig up the runway and crush the concrete to use in building Newbury bypass; 3, to re-use some of the main base buildings for warehouse and industrial use on a temporary basis until December 1997; and 4, to allow model aircraft flying on the Common. A planning brief to guide future development of the air base was made public by the council at the end of 1993.

Police and courts were not the only amenities being developed during the 1700s and 1800s. A gasworks was erected in Kings Road at the end of the eighteenth century by an individual who sold up six months later to the Gas Company. It was soon after this that the corporation gained the powers under the Newbury and Speenhamland Improvement Act of 1825 to light the town. And so it was that the evening of Thursday 29 December 1825 came to be the first time the town was lighted with gas. The rate levied for lighting, watching, paving and cleansing etc. under the Act was one shilling and ninepence in the pound. In 1809 Newbury was described in a report by William Mavor on the agriculture of Berkshire as a 'genteel rich and populous brick built town'. This same report also said that a few years before, the town was paved and lighted by voluntary subscription and that about £1,400 was raised for this purpose in one morning. It went on to say: 'No tax was imposed on the inhabitants nor was an Act of Parliament required and this sufficiently attests the public spirit of the place.' However, an entry in the diary of Samuel Purdue, parish clerk of Newbury from 1766 to 1803, for 19 December 1790 says that Newbury streets were paved then.

Fire has been responsible for the destruction of many properties throughout the Newbury area over the years. At Shaw, in 1644, the house, stables and outhouses of John Royston (the rector) were reduced to ashes. Unfortunately for him it was not until the early 1860s that the town's borough fire brigade was formed. Run by the corporation, the paid brigade ran into criticism, and in 1878, when patriotic enthusiasm ruled over England, the volunteer movement in the form of Newbury's tradesmen gave birth to a volunteer fire brigade. For a short while the two brigades ran side by side, but early the following year the paid brigade resigned and the chairman of the town's watch committee handed over the keys of the fire station. Originally the fire engine and appliances were housed in a dark, damp shed in West Mills, then in a couple of old cottages in the wharf. Within a few years of the volunteer fire brigade starting up, these cottages had been updated and converted into a new station. The first fire of any great size which the brigade had to deal with was at Mr R.J. Lovell's workshops in Albert Road in January 1891 when workshops were destroyed.

It was the following year, in 1892, that what was reported as one of the most destructive fires which had taken place in Newbury to date occurred – at the Town Mills, which by irony was owned by Albert Church, the captain

Newbury Borough Fire
Brigade in the Town Mills yard
before 1878

of the volunteer fire brigade. Mr Church, despite the fact that his property was ablaze, apparently took control of the brigade. The Town Mills were destroyed, but the fire did not spread next door to Messrs Hawkins Brewery. Two years later, in 1894, part of Newbury was flooded and the volunteer fire brigade pumped altogether an estimated 550,000 gallons of water from the cellars of the West Mills Brewery and also from several streets. In 1904 a discussion took place at a general meeting in Newbury regarding the horseing of engines. It was reported that the brigade had failed to find horses to attend a fire. A Mr Purdue, who subsequently resigned from the brigade in 1912, promised to keep a supply of horses for the future. Lack of horses was not the only thing which prevented them from attending a fire. In 1911 the brigade did not turn out to a fire because there was no water at the Compton station.

The brigade was financed by subscribers – in 1911 there were three hundred altogether. Most volunteer firemen were drawn from the immediate town area (Northbrook Street, Bartholomew Street, Mill Lane, Cheap Street, Kings Road, etc.). It was in 1913 that the brigade bought a most important addition in the shape of a motor engine – described by the *Newbury Weekly News* as the most useful appliance that had ever been brought into the fire station. At the annual meeting on 29 April 1927, a fire at Colthrop Mills, Thatcham, was mentioned as being one of the largest fires the brigade had ever attended.

Newbury volunteer fire brigade was taken over on 17 August 1941 by the national fire service. The change-over was not without acrimony. A letter from the chief officer of the late Newbury volunteer fire brigade, E. Martin, to the chief officer at the central fire station in Devizes, E. Rendell, said:

After all our boys went through during the blitzes last winter, they the ordinary part-time fire brigade have not been treated with any consideration . . . it seems very unfair to be practically left out and new men out in charge who have had very little experience with civil fires and blitzes.

Members of one of Newbury's fire service teams in Park Way during the Second World War

After the Second World War this was in turn disbanded and responsibility transferred to the local authorities, in this case to Berkshire County Council. In the 1950s a new fire station was built in Hawthorn Road. The Newbury fire brigade was involved in the Hungerford Massacre, the M4 pile-up on 13 March 1991 when ten people died, and the fire at Windsor Castle in 1992.

CHAPTER TEN

War and Peace

ewbury's citizens have played their part in military service over the years. As far back as the early sixteenth century, Newbury's best-known citizen, Jack of Newbury, gathered and equipped fifty pikemen and fifty horsemen for the king's army during a war in Scotland.

The town played an important part in the great event of the seventeenth century, the Civil War. Indeed the outcome of the first and second battles of Newbury were influential in the course of English history. In fact, for the sake of a few barrels of gunpowder, it is thought that the history of our country could well have been altered.

During the uneasy period before the outbreak of hostilities, Newbury was well placed to receive the flurry of propaganda pamphlets and broadsheets that were issued by both sides. The town was sited on major east–west and north–south routes and had important corn, wool and cloth markets that provided opportunities for an exchange of news and gossip. Newbury was not permanently garrisoned during the Civil War, but its position alongside the great road from London to Bristol ensured that it saw more than its share of military activity and temporary garrisons from both sides. Newbury was in the centre of disputed Royalist/Parliamentary territory and paid for it by being the frequent host to armies from both sides and the site of two major battles. Contrary to the support given to the king's side by many people in the rural areas, most people in the town supported Parliament, although it may be that ordinary householders simply had to support whichever army was in occupation at the time. In practice, they provided food, accommodation and stabling and were later left to tend the wounded and bury the dead.

In 1642 the quarrel of Charles I and his Parliament erupted into the horrors of Civil War. Two bloody battles were fought at Newbury, both of which are seen as among the greatest battles of the war. Charles was based at Oxford and Parliament was based in London. In the autumn of 1643 the Earl of Essex, after relieving the siege of Gloucester, was returning to London via Newbury, a town which supported Parliament, so troops were sent ahead to make arrangements for billets. But the king's troops reached Newbury first and blocked their route to the south-west of the town. The Earl of Essex arranged his men across nearby Crockham Heath. Before dawn on 20 September 1643, battle commenced and continued all day, mainly centred on the high ground of Wash Common. As night fell, each side pulled back and the king learned that expected supplies of ammunition had failed to arrive. His troops had used over eighty barrels of powder and had only ten left, hardly enough to rejoin battle the next day! The king withdrew to Oxford, and Essex continued his march to London. Accounts of

Re-enactment of the first battle
of Newbury by the Sealed
Knot Re-enactment Society at
Wash Common in 1993

the number of troops involved on each side differ and large numbers are
said to have been killed on both sides. Lord Falkland died in the battle. It is
said that a servant was able to recognize Falkland's stripped and trampled
body and had it conveyed to a nearby farmhouse at what is now Falkland
Garth on the north side of Essex Street. The body was then apparently
displayed for a while at the Guildhall in Newbury town centre, then taken to
the Bear Inn at Speenhamland from where it was carried to the family home
at Great Tew near Chipping Norton and interred at the church without a
marker.

There was no obvious reason for a battle on Wash Common, but the
arrival of the troops there goes back to Essex's decision to use the River
Kennet to protect his left flank as far back as Hungerford, after the recent
attack at Aldbourne Chase. Also the king apparently failed to reconnoitre
the ground in front of his army's position the night before the battle. It has
been said by Civil War historians that had they occupied the level ground in
front of themselves (up to the edge of Wash Common), they would almost
certainly have stopped Essex in his tracks. If this had been the case, the
Civil War may have finished there at Newbury with a victory for the king,
instead of dragging on for so much longer.

The basic topography of the land in this area is said to be much the same
after 350 years. This includes the valley which the Royalists blocked, the lanes
Essex's troops used, Crockham Heath where the Parliamentary troops were
camped, Biggs' Cottage (behind Biggs Hill) where Essex is said to have spent
the night before the battle, and Falkland Farmhouse where the body of
Viscount Falkland is said to have been first taken after the battle. The Falkland
memorial at Wash Common was unveiled on 9 September 1878 as a
monument to the battle. Precise movements, even contemporary ones, during
both the first and second battles are confused, mainly because of the lack of
effective methods of communication in the seventeenth century. There were no
maps or anything by which they could coordinate what happened. One
contemporary account, sent in a letter from the army (the king's side) to a
noble lord in 1643, said of the start of the first battle of Newbury:

A late seventeenth-century engraving by I. Lightbody representing one of the battles of Newbury 1643–4. From Clarendon's *The History of the Rebellion and Civil War in England*

The BATTLE of NEWBURY.

The next morning being Wednesday the 20 of September, by break of day (instead of the flight which upon all their former proceedings we had reason to expect), we discovered them settle in the most advantageous way imaginable of receiving us.

An article in the *Newbury Weekly News* of 17 September 1942 says that during the first battle of Newbury sixty cartloads of wounded men were taken to Newbury to be treated by the regimental surgeons.

Another of the greatest battles of the Civil War was at Newbury in October 1644, when King Charles took up a strong defensive position to the north of Newbury while he waited for other sections of his army to join battle. His troops occupied the villages of Speen, under Prince Maurice, to the west and Shaw to the north-east, and were encamped in open fields in between. The Parliamentary army, advancing from Bucklebury and Thatcham under the Earl of Manchester to attack the town from the north-east, took up positions around Clay Hill. Shaw House, the house of Sir Thomas Dolman, became famous as the scene of one of the deadliest struggles in the second battle of Newbury. It was Thomas's grandson who housed Charles I during this battle.

It was decided that a body of twelve thousand men of the Parliamentary army should undertake a night flanking march (overnight on 26/27 October), via Chieveley and Boxford, to attack the king from the west. Led by General Sir William Waller and Oliver Cromwell, a simultaneous attack would be made of the front and rear of the Royalist position. On the morning of 27 October 1644 the Earl of Manchester's army came down the hill and attempted to storm Shaw House, maybe an attempt to mask the flanking move. But it was on 27 October in the afternoon that the great battle near Shaw House took place. The king, having learned of his enemy's movements, sent Prince Maurice to entrench his men on the high ground of Speen Hill to protect the rear of his position. But Waller's forces arrived before defences were finished and drove them down through Speen. The signal for Manchester to begin his attack from the east was that a gun would be fired (when the rest of the Parliamentarians began their attack), but the signal was apparently not heard. The king's reserve eventually did attack and fighting, again around Shaw House, was intense and much blood was shed. Parliamentary troops were driven back to Clay Hill and during the night the king, unaware that at Shaw things were going his way, withdrew, leaving his crown, treasure, guns and supplies at Donnington Castle. But for better communication, the outcome of the battle might have been different. The battle has been described as indecisive, but the Parliamentarians failed in their effort to crush the king and the Royalists certainly scored a moral victory.

After the battle Cromwell and Manchester made counter accusations blaming each other for the mistakes. The New Model Army was subsequently formed, which led to Parliament winning the Civil War and the king being tried and then executed in 1649. Cromwell and the Puritans held power until monarchy was restored in 1660.

Shaw House still stands but the housing estates of Speen and Western Avenue now cover most of the ground fought over. In the panel surrounding a first-floor window there is a hole, reputed to have been made by a cannon-ball fired at Charles I on the morning of the big battle. Skirmishes had been going on already, but it is not altogether clear whether Charles was in the house at the time. The motto of the Dolmans: 'King and law shouts Dolman of Shaw' is said to have originated during the battle. Tradition has it that Dolman shouted it to the assembled troops as a kind of password.

Various relics relating to the Civil War have been found in Newbury over the years. A property in the Market Place was said to have been a noted hostelry, bearing the loyal sign of the king's head, and a rendezvous of the Royalist party in Newbury. The site is now part of the Kennet Centre, opposite Bear Lane. The king, Lord Carnarvon and Viscount Falkland are said to have lodged in this quarter the night before the first battle of Newbury. During excavations at Newbury town centre between 1971 and 1974 iron slag confirmed that iron-working must have been carried out there from the early twelfth to at least the sixteenth century. Coining was carried out in unusual places in the Civil War and it is considered possible that this area could have been used as a temporary mint.

The round barrow cemetery at Wash Common (national monument no. 12075) is believed by local tradition to cover the remains of soldiers killed in the first battle of Newbury. However, nothing was discovered during excavations of the monument between 1967 and 1969 to give positive evidence of its original purpose. It may be that the barrows were used as a focus for burials, although very few bodies may actually have been buried there. St Nicolas churchyard in Newbury was used to bury soldiers from both battles, as evidenced by entries in the churchwarden's accounts for the years ending August 1644, September 1645 and September 1646. The four barrows (one of which has been levelled) are all scheduled as ancient monuments of national importance and were among the first twenty-two sites scheduled in Berkshire under the Ancient Monuments Act before 1930.

Portraits of officers of both armies in the second battle of Newbury are now in the museum.

Early in 1993 the *Newbury Weekly News* reported that remains of what was thought to be the body of a Civil War soldier had been dug up in a field opposite St Mary's church, Speen. Pathologist Dr Robert Menai Williams at Newbury District Hospital is reported to have said that the bones (which were re-interred) probably dated back to the Civil War. Also found have been a short, bayonet-like sword and a cannon shot in a skull on Wash Common at the site of the first battle of Newbury, and a sword made into a pike-head at Speen on the site of the second battle of Newbury. What is known as the 'Cromwell' bowl, said to have been used by Cromwell when he stayed at a house called Stargroves in East Woodhay shortly after the second battle of Newbury, is now on display in Newbury Museum.

Donnington Castle, just north of the town, was besieged for twenty months during the Civil War. In 1386 Richard de Abberbury received from the young king, Richard II, a licence to 'build anew and fortify with stone and lime and crenellate a certain castle on his own land at Donyngton, Berkshire'. A 1768 map of 10 miles around Newbury, surveyed by John Willis, identifies Donnington Castle as where poet Geoffrey Chaucer spent the last couple of years before his death in 1400, aged seventy-two.

It was important, because of its geographical position, for the castle to be in the hands of a loyal subject. Henry VIII visited Donnington in 1539 and 1541 and a Privy Council was held there by his son Edward in 1551. The estate was granted by Edward to his half-sister Elizabeth, in whose honour the house was repaired and refitted in 1568 for a visit by her. At this stage a bridge was built to replace the drawbridge.

In 1643, immediately after the first battle of Newbury, Charles I seized Donnington from John Packer, the Parliamentarian, and sent Sir John Boys with a regiment to garrison the castle. He built earthworks to strengthen the castle, which is part of the outer ring of defences around Oxford.

The Parliamentarians made several attempts to capture the castle. From July 1644, for twenty months, Donnington held against the forces of

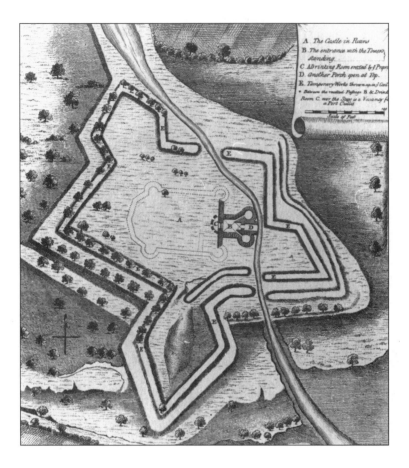

Plan of Donnington Castle,
from Grose's *Antiquities of
England and Wales*, 1773

Parliament and it was during this time that most of the structure was
destroyed, three of the towers apparently being beaten down in twelve days'
continual cannon fire. Sir John Boys only surrendered to Colonel Dalbier
when ordered to by the king on 1 April 1646 at the end of the war. Indeed,
in the midst of the quarrel between Manchester and Cromwell after the
second battle of Newbury, the king retrieved his artillery, which he had left
there after the action, from Donnington Castle. Later that year John Packer
recovered the estate and extended the Elizabethan Lodge, which became
Donnington Castle House.

Today Donnington Castle is managed by English Heritage, but the nature
of the castle's future could change. In 1992 English Heritage announced
plans to look at all the monuments of which it is guardian (and which the
nation in turn owns) to see whether it would be of benefit for some to be
locally managed (by tourist offices, trusts or councils). No one came
forward in the case of Donnington Castle and so it is still managed by
English Heritage.

The First World War had a mixed effect on Newbury. On the one hand,
organizations such as the volunteer fire brigade suffered the loss of
personnel who were called up for active service or were involved in making

Newbury Market Place. Return of local soldiers from the Boer War, 10 June 1901

munitions. Captain Barton said in his report to the brigade's annual meeting of 14 November 1916:

> The year 1916 has probably been one of the most difficult in the history of the brigade. During the year there has been one resignation, from ill health, and we have lost six more members who have been called up for military service, three recruits have come in. At the present time our establishment consists of captain, sergeant, engineer, branch man and nine men, a total of 13, a number which is quite inadequate to the needs of the town and district.

The war also had the effect of a reduction in subscriptions and donations to the Newbury Relief Committee and Guild of Social Help. It was in the report 1917–18 that for the first time the accounts showed an adverse balance of over £16.

Even Newbury racecourse played its part in the First World War. It was occupied by troops at first and was then opened for racing in 1915. From 1916 onwards it was an inspection depot for the war office and then a tank repair park, being restored to its original purpose of racing in 1919 when the war was over.

The old Didcot, Newbury and Southampton Railway provided a vital link in the war since Winchester was one of the main assembly areas for troops awaiting transport to France. From August to October 1914 passenger services were suspended and instead troop specials were run.

But the First World War had a silver lining for the town in some respects. Trade was fairly prosperous, labour was in demand and, as over the rest of the country, there was comparative prosperity for wage earners, meaning that less was paid out by the committee of the relief of the poor. Another consequence of the war was the formation by the Guild of Social Help of an infant welfare centre in Newbury.

To mark the end of the war, a United Service of Thanksgiving was held in the Corn Exchange, Newbury, on 17 November 1918. In addition, nearly a hundred local soldiers who had been prisoners of war were given a welcome home party by Newbury Women Unionists on 24 February 1919, attended by the mayor and mayoress, Mr and Mrs Adrian Hawker.

On 3 September 1939 – following the announcement that Britain was again at war – several parts of Newbury racecourse were requisitioned once more by troops. Racing, however, continued on and off until August 1942 when the racecourse became the American G45 supply depot, whereupon it became covered with concrete roads, hard standings and 35 miles of railway lines and the stables became a prisoner-of-war camp. Even after the war it continued as an army supply depot until March 1946 when the Ministry of Supply took charge of all remaining stores for disposal under the Lease and Lend Agreement with America. Stores and equipment from other areas were sold off at the racecourse and it was in June 1947 that the land, including the original course, was released and work on clearing it and turning it back into a racecourse began. It re-opened as a racecourse in spring 1949.

During both world wars, many buildings such as church halls were requisitioned for military use, sometimes for billeting troops during training. In the early 1990s, when repairs were carried out to the United Reformed church lecture hall, training booklets on gas precautions and dealing with

Military activity on Newbury racecourse during the Second World War

Home Guard of Hovis Bakeries, who owned both Town Mills and West Mills, c. 1940

incendiary bombs were found under the floorboards. There were also seven boots for left feet!

The Kennet and Avon Canal was seen as having a major defensive role across England during the war – some pillboxes remain today. Indeed the war produced activity on the canal, such as when Collier and Catley Ltd of Reading used it to transport ballast for building the pillboxes. The old Didcot, Newbury and Southampton Railway was again a vital link in the Second World War, as it had been during the First. This time all passenger services and day goods trains were suspended for eight months, from August 1942, so that the line could be doubled up in preparation for the Normandy landings in 1944. In the year leading up to D-day, up to sixteen thousand military trains used the line.

Arrangements were made early on in the war for public shelters at Victoria Park, the cattle market, the wharf and the back of the Corn Exchange. A social exchange for mothers and children was established at the Corn Exchange and arrangements were made with the YMCA, helped by a local committee, for The Plaza to be used as a social centre and entertainment venue for troops billeted in Newbury. Several schools in the area were used to house evacuees, including St Nicolas Junior C of E School and St John's Infant C of E School. As early as 2 September 1939 five hundred evacuees arrived in town. Extra baths were provided at the washhouse in the wharf for troops, and a list of lodgings was compiled by

Newbury Council for workers who were transferred to the area for work on essential war supplies.

Minutes of a monthly meeting of Newbury Council on 23 July 1940 show that the War Office had given instructions for the construction of a temporary bridge, to be used in the case of emergency only, across the River Kennet between Park Way and the wharf car park. Known by some locals as the 'American Bridge', it actually had nothing to do with the Americans! During the war, The Plaza entertainment venue was used for national registration work and for the issue of ration cards.

On 3 September 1939 Newbury District Hospital controller reported that the air raid precautions officer had authorized him to spend up to £40 on protective work at the hospital. He had been given instructions to use ten thousand sandbags from the store to be filled and placed in position by the local territorials.

Altogether 201 bombs were dropped in the Newbury area up to May 1945, although most of these were before 1941. The first air raid siren sounded on 25 June 1940 and the last on 29 August 1944. It was 25 hours after the initial alert that the first bombs fell in the Newbury district – in the grounds of Burghclere Grange, formerly Burghclere rectory. Annual summaries of alerts in the area show that there were far more alerts in 1940 and 1941 than later in the war.

St John's church sustained this damage when a bomb was dropped on Newbury during the Second World War

Only twenty-six houses in the whole Newbury area were either demolished or damaged beyond repair. An incendiary bomb was dropped on the north porch of Newbury parish church, one in Victoria Park and another in the yard of Messrs Hooper and Ashby in Bartholomew Street overnight on 6/7 November 1940. All were quickly extinguished and caused no damage.

The first death in the Newbury/Thatcham area was on 16 August 1940, when a serviceman, Colonel Urquhart, was killed during the first raid on Thatcham.

By far the most serious incident in the Newbury area was on 10 February 1943 when fifteen people died in the largest fatal casualty incident of the Second World War within the Berkshire County Council area, which then did not include Reading borough. During the raid, Newbury's third, bombs were dropped on the town and the streets were machine-gunned. As well as the eleven women and four men who died, fifteen women and ten men were sent to hospital and fifteen women and one man were dealt with at the first-aid post. So many people turned up at the bomb sites to help pull debris away that first-aiders reported that it was impossible to have silence periods to hear if there were any more people buried. The bombs hit Newbury Senior Council School, St John's church and St Bartholomew's Almshouses. The whole of Southampton Terrace at the bottom of Newtown Road had to be pulled down afterwards. And all this damage appears to have been done by a single Dornier 217 E4. Being a Wednesday, it was early closing day. Most pupils had also already gone home after school. Had this not been the case, casualties could have been higher.

wbury Senior School, which
s badly bomb-damaged
ring the Second World War

It was during an incident in March 1941 that one regular fireman and two auxiliary fire servicemen, all from the Newbury volunteer fire brigade, were killed in enemy action at Portsmouth.

During the war, the Red Cross Message Bureau had a branch at the Citizens' Advice Bureau in Newbury Library, at which they dispatched and received messages from abroad. Many of the ordinary enquiries lodged each month with the Citizens' Advice Bureau from 1941 to 1948 were directly related to wartime (evacuation, food rationing, prisoners of war).

As with other townspeople throughout the country, Germany's surrender on 7 May 1945 marked the beginning of celebrations by Newbury folk. There was a three-day Whitsun programme of festivities, beginning with a 500-strong service and a victory parade throughout the town. Decoration adorned virtually every shop front along the main roads. Even the *Newbury Weekly News* failed to appear that week, as printers joined in the celebrations.

With the news of Japan's surrender on 14 August 1945, there were bonfires in every village, dancing at the Corn Exchange, street parties and a thanksgiving service. The first victory bell in the area was rung by the vicar of Thatcham, who went straight to the church tower after hearing the news on his radio.

CHAPTER ELEVEN

In the Field and Out

Newbury's industry throughout the years has often closely followed the area's natural resources, and indeed farming has always been important and has existed even as far back as earliest man in the Newbury area.

Certainly from 1768 to 1801 agriculture was important to all around. In 1768 the town's population was 3,732 people living in 930 houses. By 1801 it had risen to 4,275 living in 965 houses. The small and scattered population consisted largely of illiterate farm labourers and as such there was still considered to be no need for a local Newbury newspaper. Papers relating to the proposed enclosure of Wash Common (1851–6) show that there were 6,379 people living in Newbury and that agriculture and general trading were the main occupations. The importance of agriculture in the town's history is depicted on Newbury's first official coat of arms, developed in 1948. The legendary Newbury Castle (see Chapter Three) serves as a crest; there are sheaves of corn to symbolize the town's agricultural connections, a teasel to represent the cloth industry, wavy lines to indicate the River Kennet and crossed swords to denote the town's two battles in the Civil War.

Now, however, although farming is still a player in the town's fortunes (particularly in the outlying villages), the last census (1991) showed that out of 69,850 people resident within Newbury, aged sixteen and over and either employed or self-employed, there were just 1,390 working in agriculture, forestry and fishing – only 2 per cent of the working population. This compares with 3.6 per cent working in farming, fishing and related occupations in 1981.

Investment by the area's inhabitants in the land in its turn gave birth to firms such as Chas. Midwinter and Son Ltd and Doltons. Charles Midwinter came to Newbury in about 1830 from Reading to be an apprentice to Shaw's seedsmen, corn merchants and market gardeners in Cheap Street. This firm grew its produce on the West Fields of Newbury and took it by horse and van to Newbury, Andover, Hungerford, Basingstoke and other markets. It was in 1860 that Chas. Midwinter took over the corn business here when Shaw's moved to Mark Lane, London, and from then on the Newbury business became known as Midwinter's, agricultural merchants.

The business began to grow when Charles's son Henry, who subsequently was a deacon of Newbury Congregational church, superintendent of a Sunday school in 'The City', mayor of Newbury in 1887 and a JP, was taken into partnership in 1869. Over the years new premises were acquired in

Queen's Road and Cheap Street. Midwinters was a well-known sight at the annual Newbury Show and won several cups for the best trade stand – one such occasion being on 22 September 1985, 125 years to the day that the business first opened its account, with a deposit at the London and County Banking Company of just over £67. In 1986 the company moved to Brook Way, the buildings now occupied by Meridian Television. However, trading conditions worsened, and in 1987 Midwinters merged with another firm to become Lidstone Midwinter Ltd, and a year later the business was sold to Berks, Bucks and Oxon Farmers Ltd. The Newbury branch was eventually closed in 1992. Five generations of the Midwinter family were involved in the business.

It is thought that Doltons was started as a market gardening business in Speenhamland in 1792, although according to Penelope Stokes in her 1992 book called *Going With The Grain* (a history of Doltons) there is no specific documentation to prove this. It was Henry Dolton, born in 1823, who expanded the business into the grain trade. After the agricultural depression of the early nineteenth century (during which local mobs apparently destroyed more than a score of machines in the machine riots of the 1830s), the industry saw the start of an economic upturn. Author Penelope Stokes said that in Newbury in 1842–3, corn sold at Newbury's market was worth £181,518, more than the figure for Reading (£153,652).

From the mid-1850s onwards, much of Henry's business was carried on from a barn known as Dolton's Storage, next to Wharf House (later known as Kendrick House where he lived with his family), where grain could be loaded straight onto barges. Other products followed – barley, specialist forage for pigeons, poultry and game – and in 1912 the business became involved in milling. That year Charles Dolton took out a lease on Shaw Mill and shortly afterwards most of the firm's business was carried out from Shaw. A few years later the company left its Corn Wharf premises for offices in Cheap Street and warehousing in Wharf Road. Shaw Mill was bought by the Doltons in the early 1950s.

Later that decade the company bought Town Mills, used by Hovis since the 1920s for flour production, and West Mills, first a granary and then a furniture store until it caught fire in 1965. At the same time Shaw Mill was sold. Bulk sales were the company's main business by now, although animal feed production was done at Town Mills. By the late 1960s Doltons was said to have been involved 'in the entire crop-growing cycle, from seed supply through cultivation to harvesting' (Penelope Stokes, *Going With The Grain*). The firm moved to larger premises at Red Shute Mill (previously known as Grimsbury Farm) in 1972, where it remains in 1994 (now known as H. Dolton and Son Ltd), having merged with Sidney C. Banks plc, of Sandy in Bedfordshire, in 1991.

Also as a result of the area's heavy involvement with agriculture, the town cattle market was opened in Market Street on 18 December 1873. It was enlarged in 1915, but closed down in 1969. As far back as 1839, on 6 December, Newbury Cattle Show and Market was held in Clements Yard on the east side of Bartholomew Street. This event may well have been the forerunner to the annual Newbury Show, held for the first or second time in December 1840 in the Market Place area by the newly formed Newbury Agricultural Society.

Newbury cattle market,
c. 1860–70

It was the area's natural resources again (this time in the form of the river
and canal) which provided the lifeforce for milling, an industry which held
its head high in Newbury for several centuries. As far back as the Domesday
Book, there were known to have been mills at Thatcham, Greenham,
Donnington, Shaw and Speen, although Newbury itself was not mentioned
specifically by name (see Chapter Two). More mills sprung up and by the
early 1400s Shaw had four or five watermills – for corn, malting, tanning
and fulling – whereas in Domesday it had just one mill. However, in
medieval times the rule was that all the corn grown on the manor had to be
ground at the lord's mill – it was the lord of the manor who owned the mill.
It was Queen Elizabeth (reign 1558–1603) who allowed the millers to deal
in grain or meal. It is not known exactly when Newbury's Town Mills or
West Mills were established, but Court of Chancery records in about 1205
show that there were two mills in Newbury, one a fulling mill. Walter
Money, in his *History of Newbury*, suggests that 'this fulling mill is no
doubt to be identified with that known as West Mills' and that the other mill
can be reasonably thought to have been the Town Mill. By the fifteenth and
sixteenth centuries many villages had their own fulling mills: for example,
Godwyn's Mill at Speen (established 1445); Sandleford Priory Mills
(thirteenth century); Colthrop Mill (1472, bought by Thomas Dolman 1557);

Hovis steamer lorry on West Mills Wharf, taking on water from the Kennet and Avon Canal

and Bagnor Mills (1590), where land adjacent is still called Rack Marsh. Fleeces from sheep grazing on the nearby Berkshire chalk downs were used to make the cloth. The abundancy of fulling mills was of course indicative of the growth and success of the town's wool and clothing industry (see Chapter Four). Part of Jack of Newbury's house still exists on the corner of Jack Street, which leads to Victoria Park, but was then called Rack Marsh or Tenter Ground because it was here that woollen cloth was pegged up by tenter-hooks and stretched to dry.

By the eighteenth century the fulling process was no longer needed for the sort of cloth Newbury made. Many mills changed their function as the need arose. For example, Colthrop Mill at Thatcham was at various times a corn mill, fulling mill and paper mill. During the First World War it supplied paper which was subsequently made into cartons by a London firm. Now cardboard, product packaging and corrugated fibreboard is made there. Other businesses such as transport and vehicle insurance research and development have also been established on the site.

By the early 1830s there were also silk and paper mills in the district. In fact, in a Municipal Boundary Commission report dated around 1837, the only manufacturers in the town of Newbury itself were said to have been paper, silk and corn mills.

Fire struck Town Mills in 1892, largely destroying it. But it was rebuilt and modernized in months. In 1921 it was sold to Hovis Ltd as a flour mill and subsequently also saw life as a place for manufacturing barley meal and animal foodstuffs. Hovis closed down in 1957 and a year later Town Mills was sold to H. Dolton and Son Ltd, who used it to process cereal seed as animal foodstuffs. In 1971 the firm offered Town Mills to the borough council, hoping it would be used as a theatre or council offices, but the council turned the offer down. The mill was demolished and in 1981 modern flats built.

West Mills was also bought by Hovis Ltd in 1921, but some time later was used by Windsor and Neate as a furniture store. Fire, however, sealed its fate in 1965 and it was eventually demolished to make way for a development of town houses called Dolton Mews. The tall block of flats close by used to be a grain silo.

Shaw Mill was converted into flats and the original mill stayed. In 1766 a great crowd marched on Shaw Mill, causing damage and throwing flour into the river. This vandalism was part of the bread riots in the town. Bakers subsequently reduced bread by tuppence and said there would be more cuts, but still the rioters marched on Shaw Mill. Greenham Mills, at Boundary Road, became the town's first electricity generating station. Flats have now been built there.

Although mainly an agricultural area, the town has also been significant in other industries too, one of them being among the oldest crafts in the world – brick-making. Locally, the clay of the Reading Beds and London clay was used and the area around Newbury and Thatcham was dotted with kilns. The Romans made flue and roof tiles at Shaw, but the craft died out when the Romans left in the fourth century and it only became a thriving industry in the fifteenth century. The oldest surviving brick building in the area is said to be Shaw House, completed in 1581. Words such as kiln and claypit or clay hill in present-day names of roads give some indication of the likely presence of past brickworks. One of the last brick and tile work sites in the area to go was the Pinewood Estate Brick and Tile Company at Hermitage in 1967, which made use of the proximity of the Newbury to Didcot railway line by having sidings for receiving coal for its kilns. The Roman Catholic church in Newbury, with its eye-catching tower, was built in the late 1920s using Pinewood bricks. Clay was also used to make tobacco pipes – two such makers are recorded at Newbury in the seventeenth century and another near Chieveley during the eighteenth century. Potteries abounded.

Many other crafts and industries have played their part in the history of Newbury, including, of course, land-based activities such as felling and barking, basket-making, tanning and peat-digging. Withies were grown in osier beds along the Kennet Valley, including at Thatcham, for making into baskets. Coppice wood from Berkshire was highly sought after and chair-making enterprises grew. It was in 1687 that chair-maker, William Parker, set up in Speen. Peat, a natural resource within the Newbury area, turned into a flourishing industry early in the 1800s. Peat was dug particularly in the moors areas and used as fuel. Wheelwrighting and carpentry were often combined. Cottage industries in villages around Newbury included straw-plaiting, soap and candle-making and silk-weaving, which became popular in about 1585 with the advent of silk stockings. Indeed villagers were much more self-sufficient within their own communities than we are today. They would make their own clothes from material spun and woven from flax grown on local farms, make their own wines and beer, and use local tanned leather to make shoes and boots, plus saddles and harnesses.

Berkshire was famous for its tanning industry, mainly because of its many oak trees. A quarter of the tree's value was contained in the bark, which was sold to leather tanners. There were several tanneries in the area – in Donnington, at Greenham and in Cheap Street. But it was a long process, which involved soaking the bark for nine to fifteen months in water before drying and finishing, and although it continued into the nineteenth century, it is now a thing of the past.

Clock and watch-making was a thriving industry in Newbury for the best part of two hundred years from the mid-1600s. There were at least a hundred clock and watch-makers in Newbury, maybe some attracted to the town by the prosperity brought about by its textile industry, coupled with its excellent geographical position which led to its importance as a coaching centre. Robert Coster, Newbury's first clock-maker, was admitted to the clock-makers' guild in 1655, and his work sometimes ended up in high circles – a brass lantern clock made by him (with a Victorian movement in place of its original) is part of the royal collection of clocks in Windsor Castle. It was given to King George and Queen Mary during the First World War and its whereabouts before that is uncertain. The mid-nineteenth century saw Coster's descendants still working as clock-makers in the area. In the main, the clock and watch-making industry in Newbury went through three distinct phases: movements were made locally up until about 1750; from then until about 1840 parts were bought from Leicester or Birmingham and finished locally; and then finally from 1840 the finished products were imported from manufacturing cities such as Liverpool, Paris and London, with the local dealer's name painted on before being sold. John Joyce, however, made his own movements until he died in 1896.

Long-case clock made by Bartholomew Flagett, *c.* 1710, in Newbury. The fine arabesque or seaweed marquetry case may also have been made in the area

Malt was an important part of the local economy, particularly during the eighteenth and nineteenth centuries. Barley was germinated in water and then heated and dried to become malt, large quantities of which were carried to London on the Kennet navigation from the 1720s. The malt was often processed locally to become beer and brewing became another economic feather in Newbury's cap. Breweries mushroomed in the mid-1800s, maybe due to an Act brought in by the Whig Chancellor of the Exchequer, Goldbourne, in 1830 to break the brewer's monopoly. Previously it was difficult for anyone to set up as a brewer, since outlets were mainly through the system of tied houses. After 1830 anyone who paid a £2 licence fee could sell beer from their own homes, although the Act was rescinded in 1869. So, whereas in 1800 there were six breweries in the town of Newbury, in 1864, if you include the surrounding towns and villages in the district, there were twenty maltsters and twenty-two brewers. Another possible indirect reason for the large number of breweries in the area could have been the impact which the coaching era had on the town. An article in the *English Illustrated Magazine* of 1888 described Speenhamland, as 'a kind of suburb of inns and posting houses which connected it with the Bath Road'.

By the time the Phoenix Brewery was founded at No. 50 Bartholomew Street in 1841, there were already eight breweries in the town. The firm was established by William Nutley and specialized in three types of beer: Berkshire Ambar (nowadays known as bitter), Stout, and Porter. In 1893 the Nutley family sold out to Herbert Finn, who was also a partner in the Steam Brewery in Ipswich. Output in 1920 was about 130,000 gallons a year, although it was one of the smaller breweries in town. It remained in the Finn family until 1923 when it was sold to Usher's Brewery in Wiltshire – from then it was used as a store until Usher's left in 1930. Now the main brewery building is empty (although Newbury Electrical Supplies occupies an outbuilding) and the Brewer's House has become the offices of James and Cowper chartered accountants. There were twenty-nine tied houses linked to The Phoenix, including The Angel at Woolhampton, The Borough Arms in King's Road, Newbury, The Globe in Bartholomew Street and The Wellington Arms. There were definite advantages to having a job at a brewery such as The Phoenix, although how workers managed to stand up straight at the end of the day is anyone's guess! Staff worked a six-day week from 5.30 a.m. to 7.30 p.m. and all except the apprentice were allowed a daily ration of beer: a pint at 6 a.m., a pint at 11 a.m., a pint at 4 p.m. and another at 7 p.m.!

Eventually larger breweries bought up the smaller ones, although after the First World War there were still four breweries in Newbury – The South Berks Brewery at West Mills and No. 17 Bartholomew Street, The Newbury Brewery in Northbrook Street, The Phoenix Brewery at No. 50 Bartholomew Street and The Speenhamland Brewery in Oxford Street. By the start of the Second World War, all were owned by either H.G. Simonds of Reading or Usher's of Trowbridge. Now there are none left.

The opening of the 18½ mile Kennet navigation (the part of the Kennet and Avon Canal which runs from Reading to Newbury) in 1723, authorized

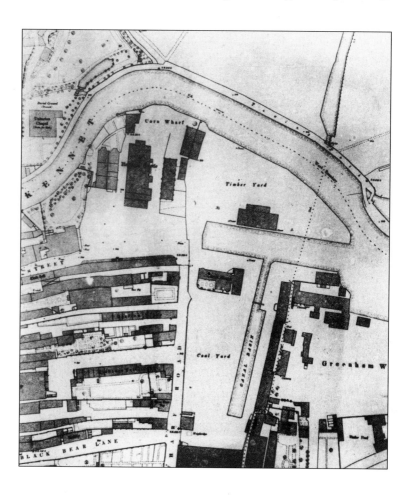

p showing the canal and
wbury Wharf as it was until
1930s

under a 1714 Act, opened up new business possibilities for the people of Newbury. And the linking of the Kennet navigation with the River Avon in Bath, which was built in sections from 1796 to 1810, took this a step further. In those early days barges carried anything from groceries to timber and coal. Tons of grain and malt were regularly taken to London. Just two of the local businesses which depended on the canal were Doltons corn mill and Plentys Ltd. There were two wharves at Newbury; one was called West Mills Wharf, which according to a publication called *Kennet Alive* published by Thames Valley Newspapers Ltd in 1990, was last used in 1950 when salt was unloaded there. The other was called Newbury Wharf and was on the site of the present car park. In the canal heyday this wharf effectively became the headquarters for trade being carried to London and the whole of the west of England. Newbury's original Cloth Hall was converted into storage for goods awaiting transport on the canal, but this wasn't enough and so a long row of granaries was built. But the demise of the canal was soon to come about, partly with the railway and partly with the motor lorry.

The Great Western Railway took over the running of the canal in 1852, but maintenance declined and tolls were levied. In 1950 the canal was declared closed for routine maintenance, with no opening date. In 1963 responsibility for the canal was taken over by the newly formed British Waterways Board. But the canal stayed closed for navigation until 1990 and is now mainly used for leisure, although the South Midland Water Transport Company (from Towcester in Northants) transports coal to Newbury, using canals.

When the town's weaving industry declined, a new spirit of enterprise started up for business towards the end of the seventeenth century. New firms, some of which survive today, started up and this spirit continued well into the twentieth century. The Newbury Savings Bank was started in 1817 and continued for over a century. The House of Toomer, ironmongers, can be said to be one of Newbury's oldest stores. It was established in 1692 by James and Sarah Toomer at No. 4 Northbrook Street and eight generations of the family have helped run the store. The store operated from its site in

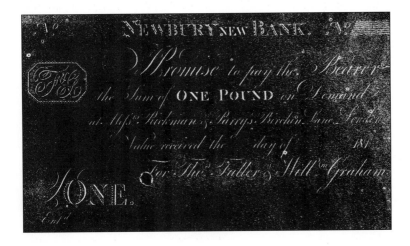

Ink proofs from die-casting plates originating from Newbury Bank

Griffin and Son Butchers, situated on the bridge next to the canal in Northbrook Street, 1905/1910. The butchers, home of the 'Newbury sausage', is one of the few businesses which still bears the same name and location

Northbrook Street for nearly three hundred years, but in 1984 moved to smaller premises in Bartholomew Street. Over the years the generations have provided the mayor of Newbury on six occasions – 1767, 1783, 1791, 1801, 1814 and (through A. Greet, Richard's father) in 1931.

Two family firms which have been prominent in the town since the early 1920s are W.J. Daniel & Co. Ltd, at No. 25 Market Place, and Camp Hopson and Co., Northbrook Street – both department stores. Daniels was started up in 1928 when Charles Daniels bought up Albert Jackson's shop. There are five branches altogether – Ealing, Windsor, Newbury and two in Wales.

Camp Hopson, born in 1921, was the result of the 'marriage' of two local businesses. One was a photography, house decorating, paper hanging, furnishing and upholstery business at No. 64 Northbrook Street and adjoining premises on the corner of West Street, which had been started by Alderman Joseph Hopson. The other was The Drapery Bazaar, which had been started by Alfred Camp from Southampton in 1886. He took over the business of Bodman and Jones which had been started by a former mayor of Newbury (1761) – William Bodman. Mr Camp had expanded his premises over the years, absorbing the drapery businesses of Messrs Payne and Vince. When the new firm of Camp Hopson and Co. opened its doors on 5 May 1921, the store stretched from Nos 6 to 14 Northbrook Street, having also taken over George Wintle's shop. In 1972 the store boasted the town's first escalator.

Another family firm which was prominent in the town until it closed in 1990 was Beynons department store, originally established in 1827. The Beynon family – first Richard and then Constance – ran it at one stage and the business was bought by Charles Summersby, MP of Shoreditch, in 1937 when he decided not to contest a further election after years as an MP and mayor of a London borough. His son Hubert subsequently ran the business for more than fifty years and Hubert's son Richard was also involved. Trade was very different in the store's heyday – representatives would travel around the villages, often with stock in their car, to take orders. Occasionally goods were given to customers on approval, a service not often found today. Prices have changed too – Mr Hubert Summersby remembers selling doormats for one shilling.

Many family-run individual shops in Newbury have now simply ceased to exist. For example, provision merchants such as Webbs in Northbrook Street and Kimber's in Pound Street, who took supplies to the gentry in country villages from the late 1800s, have long since gone. The Tudor Café, started by Jack Hole and his family in 1931, is now closed. And Davies' china shop, where McDonalds is now, has gone. This business – which sold china, glass, lamps etc. – was founded in 1847 at No. 41 Northbrook Street by James Jeremiah Davies from Reading. Several years later it moved to other premises in Northbrook Street, previously a house and now developed as McDonalds restaurant, where it remained until it closed in the 1980s. Davies' was famous locally for the grapevine which used to grow in the shop itself. The last owner was Peter Davies, who was a childhood friend of author Richard Adams who used the shop as part of the setting for his novel *Girl In A Swing*.

Other larger firms have come and gone over the years. The Newbury Public Coffee House Company, for example, started life in 1879 as the temperance movement took off and was voluntarily liquidated in 1922. The registered office was at Mansion House Street and the premises were known by various names, most recently (1903) as the Guildhall Temperance Hotel, Commercial & Family. Brass checks produced by the company and still found occasionally could be exchanged in the coffee house for non-alcoholic refreshments.

One firm which made its name as a manufacturer of household furniture was Elliotts of Newbury Ltd, originally established as Elliotts Moulding and Joinery Co. Ltd in 1895 as a specialist in high-class joinery for churches and palaces. During the First World War it made wood and metal aircraft frames, but when peace returned the firm concentrated on furniture production. In latter years it also tried its hand at designing and producing light aircraft, but the firm closed down in 1975 and its site is now occupied by Bayer, chemicals and healthcare company.

Several engineering firms made their home in Newbury earlier this century, but many have now made way for the micro-chip industries of the 1980s and 1990s. Vickers Armstrong set up several outlets in Newbury for its supermarine works as a result of the 'dispersal production' policy adopted by the company after the bombing of its Southampton factory in 1940. Detailed work and assembly was done in Mill Lane, and at Shaw they had a machine shop, press shop and engine test bed. The firm was the largest employer in Newbury during the war, with 1,400 employees. It was still operating in the area in 1960, but in 1963 closed the doors of its last factory in Newbury. Quantel, a graphics company, now stands on one of the sites occupied by Vickers.

Another engineering company, Sterling Cables, started up in King's Road around 1966 and stayed on the site until moving to Aldermaston in 1981. The firm subsequently changed its name to Sterling Greengate, but in 1990 closed there too.

One of the few remaining large engineering companies in the Newbury area is Opperman Mastergear Ltd, a gear-cutting firm which started in 1940 and has been part of the town's industrial scene ever since. It was in the mid-nineteenth century that engineer Carl Opperman from Hamburg decided to start up a business in this country. The business was handed down through the family over the years and in 1924 Opperman Gears Ltd was started up in London. Because of the company's growth it moved to Hambridge Road, Newbury, in 1940, where it produced many military products for the war effort. In 1986 Opperman Gears Ltd merged with a valve actuator manufacturer called Mastergear (also of Newbury) and is now owned by American firm Regal-Beloit Corporation.

By far the prime force in engineering in Newbury today is Plenty Ltd, which was founded in 1790 and has found fame for the name of Newbury all over the world. Founded by Southampton man William Plenty for making ploughs and agricultural equipment, the firm has been truly innovative. Today the firm employs about 320 people. It uses computer-aided design and supplies pumps and filter equipment to the gas and oil industries, but there have been ventures into many other areas too. In 1816 Plenty's first lifeboat, called *The Experiment*, was launched on the Kennet and Avon Canal at Newbury. At this time the town was a busy 'port', being linked to both west and east coasts with the opening of the canal system. By 1824 eleven of the fourteen lifeboats stationed in Great Britain were built by Plenty.

In 1863 the company produced its first marine steam engine – something it was famous for well into the present century – and in 1885 it built steam

The former iron Thatcham bridge, built and erected by Plenty Ltd. This bridge has now been replaced

machinery for Nordenfeldt submarines. It was shortly before this, in 1878, that Plenty's built and erected the original iron bridge over the Kennet, near Thatcham railway station (it has only recently been replaced). Just twenty years later, when Cold Ash clergyman Professor J.M. Bacon made his ballooning ascent of nearly 3 miles at the beginning of the sport, Plenty's provided the gas booster and other parts.

Ten years or so later and it was into another form of transport – motor transport. The company embarked on a project which did not take off – it built what is commonly called 'The Newbury Van'. The Plenty Petrol Engine Delivery Van, to give it its real name, had solid tyres and cost £225 and a new company called Stradling and Plenty was formed to market the vehicle. The motor van was available with a driver for a week's free trial. However, just a few were made and sold and the company began to give priority to its dominant marine engine business. About thirty years ago Plenty moved from its original site in Cheap Street, where the Kennet Mall shopping centre is now built, to its present site in Hambridge Road. The company used to have an iron foundry called the Eagle Iron Works in King's Road, where its castings were made. Plenty is now owned by Booker McConnell plc, a food-processing company.

Now, although agriculture and engineering are still important, the 1980s and 1990s have seen computer and other new technology companies make their homes in or around Newbury too – for example, Norsk Data Ltd, the Vodaphone group, Micro Focus Ltd and Quantel Ltd. Who knows where this micro-chip age will take our industries in the next century?

CHAPTER TWELVE

Newbury at Play

A hostelry may have existed as early as 1223 on the site where, in the mid-fifteenth century, a drinking house in Northcroft Lane, Newbury, was established by Winchester College for students and travellers between Winchester and New College, Oxford. Title deeds of another inn, the Jack of Newbury Inn in Northbrook Street, go back as far as 1754, although the property may have existed before that. On 12 October 1896 it was purchased by Thomas Brennan Manning of Henley for £5,500 freehold, subject to a loan of £5,000 being obtained at 4.5 per cent interest. Just twenty-four years later the same premises were sold by Hilda Theodora Manning and Florence Annie Manning, both spinsters, to the South Berkshire Brewery Company Limited for £3,000 – considerably lower than the price paid in 1896. By 1925 many of the inn's customers were motorists – a report by Messrs Dreweatt and Watson, estate agents and surveyors, said that the property, with its five-store stable, loft, plus garaging for three or four cars, had entirely inadequate garage accommodation because of the large proportion of the hotel custom that was generated from motorists. In the 1990s the town still has many public houses and hotels.

Festivities in the street, particularly those celebrating royal occasions, have also played a large part in the town's history. Back in 1660 bonfires are said to have blazed in the town, church bells rung for two days and the townspeople were treated to free cakes, ale and wine – all to celebrate the restoration of the monarchy following the Civil War. Local children were treated to a mammoth feast in the Market Place on the celebration of Queen Victoria's Golden Jubilee on 21 June 1887. Coronation celebrations were also held in the town many times throughout the years – for example in 1902 (for Edward VII) and in 1911 (for George V), when bells were rung in St Nicolas parish church as early as 6 a.m. Bells also sounded in 1937 on the coronation of George VI and in 1953 on the coronation of Queen Elizabeth II. Street parties were prevalent for many of the festivities, including the Silver Jubilee celebrations of Queen Elizabeth II on 7 June 1977.

As early as the sixteenth century sporting activities were on the leisure scene in the town. Newbury Bowling Club was founded in 1598 in Speenhamland. No records exist for the precise whereabouts of the club, but in those days most bowling grounds were behind pubs. Membership has waxed and waned over the years and the club was fully resurrected in the nineteenth century. In the early 1930s it moved to Victoria Park, where it still is. The clubhouse was rebuilt when it was burnt down in 1986. Originally in Newbury, as in many other places, bowling was an upper class

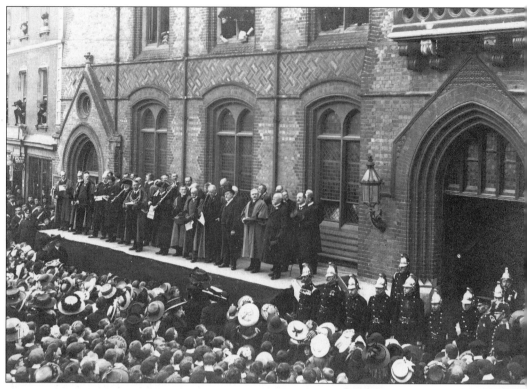

ewbury and Speenhamland
owling Club, *c.* 1865

form of entertainment, but in the late 1800s it became available to the general masses, although there has never been any restriction on entry. In the early stages there were no separate men's or women's teams – it was a completely integrated activity. The Fairhurst Cup, traditionally played between Newbury Bowling Club and Newbury Conservative Club, was first presented by Colonel James Ashton Fairhurst back in the 1930s.

The growth of the coaching era in the eighteenth century led to the birth of entertainment for the industry's guests. Coaches ran from London to Bath, making overnight stops in Newbury. Inns, which proliferated in the eighteenth century, came in very handy for this purpose. Many local inns – including the George and Pelican Inn at Speenhamland, The Bear Inn, The Chequers, The Bacon Arms, The Castle, The White Hart and The Globe – were said to be patronized by the travellers. It is not known exactly when professional theatre arrived in Newbury, but on 19 February 1787 the *Reading Mercury* mentioned it as being on a site in Northcroft Lane, which later gave way to the Temperance Hall. It was only in 1788 that an Act of Parliament was passed which allowed theatrical presentations – until then they were held illegally. The manager of the Newbury Theatre in 1787 was Henry Thornton, who continued doing the job for thirty years. In 1802 a new theatre, sometimes called the Pelican Theatre, was built in Gilder's Square, just off the Oxford Road. Its last performance was in 1843, but the building remained until it was demolished in 1976.

However, in the early 1960s local lad David Collins, with the support of his mother Judy Collins, began work on creating, from a derelict watermill at Bagnor, what is now considered to be one of the smallest and most beautiful professional theatres in the country. The building dates from 1830 and was used as a corn mill, a fuller's mill and a fine paper mill before its first season as a professional theatre in 1967. Since 1981 attendance at the Watermill, under the artistic direction of Jill Fraser, has grown. In 1992–3, 50,611 people attended performances, whereas only 25,968 went in 1982–3.

pposite above: Proclamation
the accession of King
:eorge V, outside the Town
all, 1910. *Below:* Royal
lebrations on Jubilee Day
35, at Battle Road, Newbury

Newbury's Pelican Theatre, built in 1802. It was demolished in 1976

Racing has been part of the town's history for many years. At the beginning of the eighteenth century races were held annually on Enborne Heath, with the race week being the event of the year. The corporation of Newbury is said each year to have given a cup, value £50, for the occasion. It was after a chance meeting in Newmarket's High Street between trainer John Porter and King Edward VII, for whom he trained horses, that a licence for Newbury racecourse was granted by Royal Decree. Porter had tried unsuccessfully for a couple of years to get the Jockey Club to allow such a licence. The racecourse was floated as a limited company with an authorized share capital of 2,000 £100 shares (although 1,900 were actually used) and has never had any further capital injection. It was on 26 September 1905 that the first race meeting under Jockey Club rules was held at Newbury racecourse, on land owned by Mr Lloyd H. Baxendale. The race, with a prize of 103 sovereigns and a silver cup valued at 25 sovereigns, was won by a horse called Copper King, owned by Mr D.J. Pullinger, ridden by C. Trigg.

Racing at Newbury, the second youngest racecourse in the country, was interrupted during both world wars. The Hennessey Cognac Gold Cup Chase, the second oldest-established sponsored race in the country, takes place at Newbury, which was the location during 1991 for much of the filming of the BBC television series *Trainer*. Racing is allowed on twenty-eight days of the year and the course has the benefit of its own railway station – built early on in the racecourse's life – and its own airstrip – opened in 1991. Latest additions include a £10 million remodernization of facilities such as stands, jockeys' hospital, weighing rooms and a venue for business conferences and wedding receptions, bringing it up to date on health and safety legislation. Leisure extras include pitch and putt and a golf driving range. But chief executive Major General David Pank's future plans mean turning the racecourse into a general leisure facility for the 1990s – by mid-1994 he is aiming for an eighteen-hole golf course and a health suite (to include tennis, swimming and gymnasium).

Other entertainments which existed in the area in the eighteenth century included an annual picnic for chimney sweeps (organized by Mrs Elizabeth Montagu at Sandleford Priory), Newbury Cattle Show, and of course drinking – at the end of Victoria's reign Newbury had six breweries and numerous public houses.

By the end of the nineteenth century many more leisure activities were available. People with a particular interest got together since there was no radio, television or cinema and so there was a proliferation of clubs during this period. A Literary and Scientific Institute was formed in 1843 to promote the intellectual improvement of the townspeople and the Newbury Field Club, which still exists, was founded in 1870 as 'an association for the investigation of natural history and antiquities of the district'. A club which was formed for young men, many working in local businesses, was the Guildhall Club, which was born in 1886 and died in 1969. Its first president was a keen balloonist, J.M. Bacon, a clergyman who lived at Cold Ash. Political clubs were also in existence – with the Liberals in Bartholomew Street, Labour in Northcroft Lane and the Conservatives in Cheap Street.

Musical interest groups were also on the increase – church choirs were prolific. There were ecclesiastical orchestras, and local musicians were in frequent demand at gentlemen's houses in the area. The Godding family at one time had five family members in the post of organists in and around Newbury. Various musical clubs sprang up – the Newbury Amateur Musical Society, the Newbury Amateur Orchestral Union (formed in 1879 out of a 'scratch orchestra' for a volunteer fire brigade entertainment), the Men's Choral Union, Newbury Choral Society and Newbury Town Band.

In 1870 the corporation provided a bathing-house in Northcroft (open during the summer from 6 a.m. until dusk) and sporting groups were also appearing in quick succession – Crookham Golf Club (1873), Newbury Bicycle Club (1878), and Newbury Angling Association (1880). The Newbury Gymnasium was shut in 1877 due to lack of enthusiasm, but was revived in the early 1890s. Other clubs also came and went during the Victorian era, including Newbury Working Men's Club and Institute (established in 1865 and disbanded in 1872).

In 1890 Newbury Arts Society was formed by local artists to exhibit their work, but was halted in 1914 by the First World War. Another group was not formed until after the Second World War – Newbury Art Group started in 1947 and was disbanded in 1983. The town's Corn Exchange, built in 1862 but disused in the late 1980s and early 1990s for safety reasons, has been used for many things including religious services, grain trading in the days of the cattle market (ceased in 1969) and a variety of leisure purposes. It was re-opened in 1993 after renovation and attracts entertainers of national reputation.

It was not until the second half of the nineteenth century that Newbury was able to support a newspaper of its own. Several attempts were made in the mid-1850s, but it was in 1861 that the *Newbury Weekly News* was launched by two young men working for a printer called James Blacket in his Northbrook Street printing shop – his eldest son Walter Blacket and an

Laying of the foundation stone of Newbury's library, 28 June 1905

apprentice called Thomas Turner. Printed initially by hand, the paper cost 1½d., but by the start of the twentieth century it was printed on gas-powered machinery and its cost had dropped to 1d.

Funds totalling £2,000 from American philanthropist Carnegie helped set up the town's library (although the Guildhall Club had its own library) in 1905 under the Free Libraries Act. The library opened in 1906.

Another important development in the town's leisure facilities has, of course, been the canal. The Kennet and Avon Canal was finished in 1810, including the construction of the 29-lock Caen Hill flight of locks at Devizes, Wiltshire. Back as far as the 1930s there were a few pleasure craft going through Newbury, but leisure only really took off with the introduction in 1948 of rowing boats and canoes from nearby Victoria Park. This venture continued until the early 1980s when its then owner John Gould retired. The canal itself was re-opened by the queen in August 1990 after many years of restoration by the owners British Waterways. It had not effectively been open for navigation since the early 1950s when it was closed for maintenance. Now boat trips are run throughout the summer along the canal through Newbury. Since 1973 a popular event along the 8½ miles between Hungerford and Newbury each year has been the Crafty Craft Race, which has many of its entrants wearing fancy dress while paddling their hand-built craft along the course to Victoria Park.

By the early 1900s the cinema had became a popular form of entertainment and amateur dramatic societies were also flourishing. Alfred Camp, the mayor, performed the opening ceremony of the town's first cinema, in Cheap Street opposite the railway station, in November 1910. Prices were 3d., 6d. or 9d. (1d. or 2d. for children). It was the brainchild of local eccentric Jimmy Tufnail, who had arrived in Newbury from Reading in 1887 with 7d. in his pocket after paying his fare. A rival, the Picture Palace, opened next to the Northbrook Street Methodist church twenty-six years later and closed in 1931 (Tufnail's cinema had closed in 1920). Another cinema (the Carlton) opened opposite the post office and burned

A regular visitor to the Newbury Steam Funtasia – the 1893 Tidman Steam Gallopers

down in 1950, and there was also the Regal cinema, built in Bartholomew Street in 1927 and demolished in 1968–9. In 1994 just one cinema remains – the Cannon (as it is now known), built in Park Way in 1939. But even the future of this cinema is uncertain. A Newbury District Council planning brief for the whole Park Way area has marked the cinema site for redevelopment, with the hope that a new cinema would be started elsewhere in the area. But this is now on hold and it is thought that only part of Park Way will be redeveloped in the near future.

Twentieth-century leisure developments of note in Newbury include the first youth centre in Berkshire (built on the site of the old waterside chapel next to the Kennet), the formation of a twin-town association, the annual Newbury Steam Funtasia, Newbury Community Theatre (whose first play in 1984 was all about the Newbury Martyrs), and the Newbury and Royal County of Berkshire Show. The original Newbury Show was started as far back as 1840 (see Chapter 11), but the current Newbury Agricultural Society was formed in 1909 and its first Newbury Show was held on 28 September 1909 at Enborne Gate Farm. Breaks occurred for both world wars plus an eight-year pause because of lack of support, but since 1946 the event has been held at Elcot Park, Henwick Court, Siege Cross and, since 1984, at its permanent showground at Priors Court. The event is now known as the Newbury and Royal County of Berkshire Show.

Numerous clubs have grown up in the twentieth century to meet the public's increased leisure time. Newbury Rugby Club, whose first president was Colonel James Ashton Fairhurst (grandfather of the 1990s landowner Jim Fairhurst), was formed in 1928 at Newbury Grammar School, moving after three years to its own ground in Newtown Road. The club is hoping to move to a new leisure site in Monks Lane since a business park is planned for its Pinchington Lane premises. Newbury Boys' Club held its first annual summer camp in 1947, while food rationing was still prevalent. Newbury Bowmen started in 1957 and in 1978 The Arts Workshop was launched in what was the old Temperance Hall (rebuilt at a cost of £1,250 and then opened in 1875 on the site of a 1722 school). The town's football club was formed in 1887.

Today the list of leisure activities available to Newburians is extensive: West Berkshire Ramblers, Newbury Athletic Club, Newbury Coin and Medal Society, Newbury Cricket and Hockey Club (facing problems of a pavilion at Northcroft which is in bad shape), Newbury and Crookham Golf Club, Rotaract Club of Newbury, Donnington Valley Hotel and Golf Course and Newbury Netball League to name but a few. Newbury Cricket Club formed in 1945 out of an amalgamation of Westwood and Great Western; Newbury Hockey Club formed in 1952; in 1976 the Cricket and Hockey Clubs merged. During the 1980s several hotels, each with their own health and fitness clubs, sprang up. Until 1993 the town was also home to the famous international Icicle Balloon Meets, which took place annually from 1973 at Marsh Benham. Nearby, the present Highclere Castle, built (by the third Earl of Carnarvon in 1842) of Bath stone around the previous red-brick Georgian house, was opened to the public in 1987. It has been the setting for many films and television series, including *Duel of Hearts*, *Jeeves and Wooster* (second and third series) and *Poor Little Rich Girl*. Another twentieth-century event, the Michaelmas Fair, is held at Northcroft in the form of a funfair, although it originated as a Hiring Fair in the Market Place sometime between 1627 and 1752. One of the most recent private developments is a bowling alley in Lower Way, Thatcham.

Newbury District Council has also played an important part in recreation provision in the district. Included under its control are allotments, commons (such as Bucklebury), summer play schemes, and parks (Victoria Park, Northcroft Park and Greenham House). The council has set up several sports centres (many of them joint managed with other authorities), a grants scheme to village halls, parish councils and sports clubs, and a scheme called rural recreation which takes activities to far-flung villages.

One of the bright spots in Newbury's arts calendar in the twentieth century is the Newbury Spring Festival, founded in 1978 by the Countess of Carnarvon and John Wright. Over the years many artists – musicians, painters and sculptors – with international reputations have taken part, including Sir Yehudi Menuhin, Paul Tortelier and Tom Coates. In 1992 the festival, first held in May 1979, expanded from ten to fifteen days.

CHAPTER THIRTEEN

Where Do We Go from Here?

Much has changed in Newbury throughout the twentieth century. For a start the population has grown dramatically – to 136,700 in 1991. Almost everything else has changed too, from transport to education, from health care to housing, from work to play.

Indeed life for Newbury residents has changed greatly. Former librarian Helen Purvis, who moved to Wash Common in 1927, said:

> It's not the same town as when I first moved here. We didn't have the possessions, the means of getting around – we seemed to live in a much smaller world.

Northbrook Street, Newbury,
. 1865-70

But we had in some ways a better quality of life. Life was easier in a way. In those days the grocer and other tradesmen would take your order one day and deliver what you wanted a couple of days later.

There were far fewer people about and it was a much safer world, especially for children. Newbury itself is a different place altogether – it was a little quiet country market town. There weren't many motor vehicles and things were more community based. People lived in flats over the shops and offices in the town centre and it had that warm, friendly feeling of people living there. People are more self-contained now.

And what of the future? What is in store for Newbury residents? In 1991 there was what was termed a 'political earthquake' when Liberal Democrats swept to power in the Newbury District Council elections, doubling their number of seats to twenty-four and giving them a four-seat majority over the Conservatives. The *Newbury Weekly News* reported that Newbury's dramatic election result ranked among the top ten swings against the Conservatives in the 369 district and borough council contests in England and Wales. Liberal Democrat David Rendel was elected to Newbury District Council in 1987 and returned in 1991. He also became the town's MP in May 1993 when he won the by-election caused by the death of the town's

Aerial shot of Newbury town centre showing St Nicolas church, the Town Hall and the Kennet and Avon Canal, 1986

The Jubilee clock, horse
trough, gas lamps and Russian
cannon in The Broadway,
c. 1910

Conservative MP, Judith Chaplin, by whom he had been defeated in the
general election of 1992.

Mr Rendel said:

> During the last two decades Newbury has expanded much more
> quickly than most Newburians would have liked. The old market-
> town atmosphere has almost gone. In its place has grown up a
> thriving commercial centre – thriving at least until the 1990s
> recession. Over the next few years I believe that the pace of
> development will be far slower and that this will be greatly to
> Newbury's benefit. The town will remain a centre for smaller
> businesses rather than for multi-national corporations. Meanwhile the
> bypass will at least temporarily bring some relief from the worst of
> Newbury's traffic problems. The changes we will see will be mainly
> in the fields of recreational and other facilities for those who live here

now. The rapid influx of new residents from other parts of the country will die away. In spite of all that has been lost, Newbury will remain a pleasant and sought-after place to live. It has a great future before it so long as we are determined to protect it from the overdevelopment of the recent past.

New forms of transport have brought with them changes over the years. And with the emphasis back on roads again (first it was roads, then the canal, then the railway), more changes in Newbury's road system seem likely. Plans for the future include, in 1995–6, widening of the A4 from the Robin Hood roundabout to Turnpike Road into dual carriageway (£7.1 million at 1993 prices); in 1995–6 a £4 million Thatcham Northern Distributor Road from Turnpike Road across fields, along the existing Bowling Green Road and linking with the new Dunstan Park roundabout (mainly to serve housing to the north and north east of Thatcham); in 1997–8 a combined £2.5 million road, canal and river bridge at Thatcham and two more schemes, both Department of Transport. One is for massive changes to the motorway junction at Chieveley, due to start before 1996. Two routes, known as the red route (costing £18.7 million) and the blue route (costing £19.2 million) were put forward. DoT officials say the present M4 roundabout (linking the A34) will become a bottleneck when Newbury's new bypass is built and so it is essential to take long-distance traffic away from the already busy roundabout. The red route was chosen (much to the relief of Newbury showground organizers since the blue route would have cut across their car park) and means that A34 north–south traffic will go west of the Stakis Hotel, through a tunnel under the A4 and then rejoin the A34. The second scheme is the long-awaited and much-needed Newbury bypass, due to start in 1994. Many proposed routes were considered, including several through the centre of Newbury and several eastern bypass routes. After an initial public inquiry in 1988, a western route was chosen (expected to cost £50 million, according to an article in the *Reading Evening Post* in 1991), with a few modifications. A second public inquiry was held in March 1992 to consider the new proposals relating to the compulsory purchase of land. Work on the bypass will take fifteen years to complete.

Health care has also changed over the years. Before the advent of hospitals, charities frequently took on the role of caring for some of the sick. Newbury District Hospital opened in Andover Road in 1885 and the former Union Workhouse became Sandleford Hospital in 1930. Now another change seems possible and Newbury District Hospital's future on its present site is in doubt. Plans are underway to build a new hospital for the district. Until early 1994 it was planned for a greenfield site bordered by Turnpike Road, Fir Tree Lane and the A4 Bath Road between Newbury and Thatcham. Outline planning permission has been granted for the new £12.5 million hospital – the start date is expected to be before 1996.

The final say on whether the hospital goes ahead rests with the Oxford Regional Health Authority, which in early January 1994 was still keen to build on the site, but the scheme depends to a large extent on the success of a development deal. Newbury District Hospital would be sold to local building firm Trencherwood, as would Sandleford Hospital, and houses

London Road, Newbury, 1905

would be built on both sites. Houses are also earmarked for land at Wash Water (south of Newbury), which belongs to the Newbury Hospital Helpers' League and Enborne Parish Council. The league land was bequeathed for the benefit of the health service by Miss Rosemary Rooke. But Newbury's director of development services, Alan Jones, says that planning permission is unlikely for the houses at Wash Water and the parish council has said it will not sell for development.

But at the end of January 1994 the *Newbury Weekly News* announced that the West Berkshire Priority Care Trust – which owns both Newbury hospitals – preferred Sandleford as the site for the new hospital.

There have been many twentieth-century leisure developments of note in Newbury and as the town prepares to enter the twenty-first century almost every kind of leisure activity imaginable is available within travelling reach. Furthermore, a joint scheme is planned between Newbury District Council, Thatcham Town Council and Berkshire County Council for organized sports on Henwick Field (due to start in 1994).

Property is one area of tremendous growth in the area, especially since the war. New housing estates have sprung up, latterly around Thatcham, and still more are planned. Despite the depressed property market of the late 1980s and early 1990s, prices are still vastly different to what they were, for example, in 1953 just after the coronation. Then, £1,600 would buy you a three-bedroomed, semi-detached house in Newbury and £2,950 would get you a three-bedroomed, detached house between Newbury and Thatcham. In 1994 the prices are more likely to be around £63,000 to £75,000 for the semi and £80,000 to £120,000 for the detached.

Many would say, however, that the path of progress has had its price – many old buildings have gone, to be replaced by more modern structures, although fine examples of pre-nineteenth-century architecture have been discovered this century. In 1906, while structural alterations were being carried out to a shop in the Market Place, beautiful oak panelling and deeply moulded beams belonging to the Perpendicular period of the fifteenth century were found. The wooden ceiling from the house is in the possession of Newbury Museum, not on display. Documents relating to the house go back to King Henry VIII's time, when a long-bow-string maker occupied the premises. A stone slab, part of the long-bow-string maker's equipment, is said to have been removed from the house and is now in St Nicolas churchyard.

Part of the Tudor house occupied by Jack of Newbury and his cloth factory still exists in Northbrook Street. In addition, there is the stately residence of Shaw House, built in the reign of Queen Elizabeth I by wealthy clothier Thomas Dolman. An oak staircase, dating from about 1660 and contemporary with the building itself, can be found inside Newbury's present-day Camp Hopson department store in Northbrook Street. The staircase leads up from the china department. It is said to be the only example in the town of any importance of work from the Charles II period.

The exact date of the building of the Georgian Gothic house of Donnington Grove is unknown but is probably around 1770. The Grove originated only as a place name – 'The Priors Grove' was mentioned in a grant back in 1570 and the River Lambourn flows through this land. The house itself was built by James, half-brother of Joseph Andrews (who married Anne Penrose, daughter of the rector of Newbury). In 1782 the house was sold to Beau Brummell's father. Beau Brummell was an English dandy and a friend of George IV. In the early 1990s the Donnington Grove estate was bought by the Japanese and turned into an exclusive country club and golf course.

In 1994 the country as a whole has still not recovered from a deep-seated recession which has been described by economists as the worst since the 1930s. In the 1980s Newbury was the kind of place which epitomized everything the Thatcher government stood for. New companies, particularly those involved in new technology, were flocking to the town. But in October 1993 unemployment stood at 6.3 per cent. For Sale or To Let signs on empty shops and offices are no strangers to the town.

The amount of industrial and commercial floorspace grew dramatically between 1976 and 1992. In 1976 there were 48,450 square metres of offices, 343,830 of industry and 382,120 of warehousing. The boom years of the 1980s meant that by 1992 that figure had grown to 181,720 square metres of offices, 645,240 of industry and 500,530 of warehousing. But the town has previously turned its fortunes around (after the decline of the wool trade), and there is every belief that it will do so again. A planning convention at the end of 1993 was told that if the Thames Valley is to regain its former pre-eminent position as one of the country's most important concentrations of 'high-tech' manufacturing and services, concerted effort is required from both public and private sectors, with less rigid planning policies. The difference now though is that the whole of the country, and indeed Europe, is affected – the town's fortunes are no longer solely in its own hands.

So what is the shape of development to come in Newbury? From 1945 to 1990 in Berkshire the urban spread increased by 63 per cent – that's 12,200 hectares. The district's attractive rural and urban areas are under constant pressure, according to the council's planning handbook. It adds that the location makes it attractive to business and its beauty makes it attractive to people wanting to set up home here. The handbook also says that in recognition of its character and history, much of Newbury town centre has been designated as a Conservation Area in order to protect and enhance the

Demolishing homes in King's
Road, Newbury, to make way
for a Sainsbury's store,
November 1993

existing environment. Planning policies have been drawn up to give
guidance on what development will be acceptable throughout the district.
Both the Newbury District Plan (from 1986 to 1996) and the Berkshire
County Council Structure Plan (from 1988 to 1996) are adopted documents
(approved by the secretary of state for the environment) and are designed to
be read together since the local plan applies policy to the ground. The
Berkshire Structure Plan allowed for The Moors and Siege Cross
developments in Thatcham. Berkshire County Council has now produced a
review of the county structure plan (from 1991 to 2006), which ran into
trouble late in 1993. The county council proposed 35,670 homes throughout
Berkshire (including 7,970 for Newbury district), but a panel appointed by
the secretary of state thought it should be 48,000 homes. At the beginning of
1994 Newbury District Council was reviewing its local plan, due to be
published mid-1994. The council issued a request to developers for a list of
potential development sites. As a result about eighty have been put forward
for consideration, including 1,700 homes on the Sutton Estates between
west of Newbury and the proposed bypass, and 250 homes near the
racecourse.

WALKING TOUR

1. Cloth Hall or Cloth Factory
2. Victoria Park
3. Cannon Cinema
4. Site of old Pelican Theatre
5. Clocktower
6. Newbury Bridge
7. St Nicolas church
8. John Kimber's almshouses
9. Phoenix House
10. 'The City'
11. St John's church
12. Litten chapel
13. Council offices
14. Newbury library
15. Corn Exchange
16. Town Hall or Mansion House

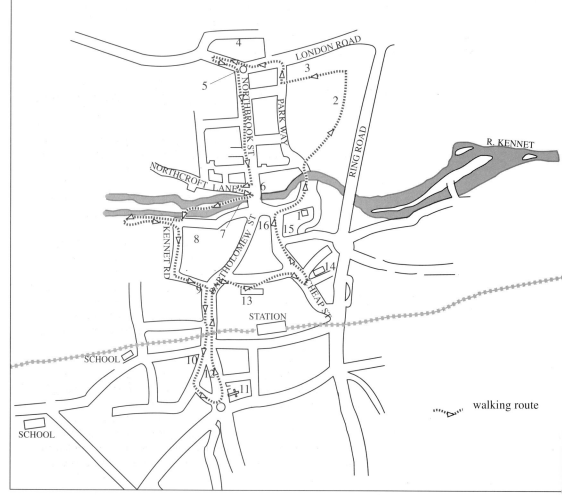

Map of Newbury Walking Tour

Newbury: from the Canal to 'The City'

This walk begins at Newbury Wharf car park near the Kennet and Avon Canal. In a circular route it takes in the key points in the Newbury centre, including the haunts of the old coaching era, the canal and one of the prettiest parts of the town – the famous 'City' area. It should take approximately an hour and a half and is suitable for wheelchair users. Throughout this walk, route instructions are given in bold type.

Keep the canal on your left.

The cream part of the long building on your right is known as the Cloth Hall or Cloth Factory. It was built in 1626 as a workhouse when wealthy clothier John Kendrick left £4,000 in his will to the corporation of Newbury to 'set the poor to work' in the clothing trade. At various times also called The Castle or The Hospital, the building has served a variety of uses over the years – including the housing of a corporation (or bluecoat) school.

The clothing industry began a terminal decline in the seventeenth century. But with the advent of the Kennet navigation from Reading to Newbury in 1723 and the Kennet and Avon Canal (to link the Kennet navigation with the Avon navigation) in 1810, Newbury Wharf area took on a new lease of life, with goods being carried to and from London. The original Cloth Hall was converted into storage, and the long row of granaries attached was built for extra storage. The Cloth Hall was repaired by public subscription as a memorial to Queen Victoria in 1902 and today houses Newbury Museum and the Tourist Information office.

Facing you are the public conveniences. This is where the canal basin used to run. To the left, next to the canal, you will see the building of the Kennet and Avon Canal Trust. Local opinion says that this stone building is built from the remains of the legendary twelfth-century Newbury Castle. Until recently local residents and even archaeologists and historians believed the castle had been in the wharf area. But a survey in 1990, in advance of a proposed wharfside development (now shelved), failed to come up with any evidence of even a 'motte and bailey' type castle, let alone a structural castle.

Storage barn at Newbury
Wharf in the 1930s.
Pictured is Mr Smith,
timekeeper and weighbridge
attender. The barn has since
been demolished

**Turn northwards now, facing the canal, and walk over the canal via
the bridge.**

This bridge was built as a temporary measure only during the Second World
War, but has remained in place ever since.

**Descend the steps, on the other side of the bridge, into Victoria Park
and go along the park's central path. If you are disabled, continue
along the path on the bridge and after about 50 yards you will see
another park entrance on the right.**

WEST MILLS & RIVER, NEWBURY.

Bygone days – a 1906
postcard of the West Mills
and river

Victoria Park was originally rough, common land, which used to be called The Marsh because of its marshy characteristic. It was created as a park in the Victorian ages (two avenues of lime trees were planted in 1883), although it had been used for public occasions before that. The name of Victoria Park was given as a tribute to Queen Victoria following her death in 1901. It was acquired by the borough by Act of Parliament in the mid-1920s and was later improved by Newbury Borough Council when it built the adjacent Park Way in 1936. At the end of this path, on the left, is a statue of Queen Victoria, guarded by two lions. On 1 February 1966 this was moved to the park from Greenham House gardens (and it had been moved there from Market Place in 1933). Two other lions, which also used to guard Her Majesty, went to the Child Beale Wildlife Park near Pangbourne. The complete statue had been erected in Newbury Market Place in 1904.

Take the second left fork at the end of the path, which leads around the edge of the park. Once out of the park, turn right into Park Way.

About 100 yards or so on the right-hand side you will see Newbury's only remaining cinema – the Cannon cinema, built in 1939. The town's first cinema, the idea of local eccentric Jimmy Tufnail, was opened in 1910 in Cheap Street opposite the railway station.

At the end of Park Way, turn left into London Road.

You are now walking the route used by the many horse-drawn coaches making their way from London to Bath in the heyday of the coaching era in the eighteenth century. On the right-hand side, about 50 yards further on, you will see Pelican Lane. Much of this area has been redeveloped now. Back in the very early nineteenth century a theatre was built between Oxford Street and Pelican Lane. It was a well-known haunt for travellers.

At the junction of London Road with Northbrook Street and Oxford Street you will see Newbury's clocktower, built in 1929.

Bear right into Oxford Street.

Along this stretch of road – London Road and Oxford Street – there were many inns in the days of the coaching era, used by travellers making overnight stops. Two of these – The Chequers and the Bacon Arms – are on the right-hand side in Oxford Street.

Turn around and head back towards the clocktower. Turn right along Northbrook Street.

You are now in an area called The Broadway. After about 100 yards on the right-hand side you will see Newbury Methodist church, built in 1837 and renovated in 1990 when new premises were opened next to the church, celebrating 250 years of Methodism in the area and combining five churches.

About 100 yards further along Northbrook Street, on the left-hand side, you will see a building with herringbone brick. This is all that remains of the house of Newbury's most famous citizen, Jack of Newbury, on the corner of Marsh Lane. Jack was famous for being a wealthy clothier at a time when the town was of national importance. The cloth factory he set up stretched from Northbrook Street right back to The Marsh.

Just across the road from Jack of Newbury's house, a passageway leads to the United Reformed church – formed in 1972 when the Congregational church joined forces with the Presbyterian church and later in 1981 a smaller sect called The Churches of Christ.

Slightly further along Northbrook Street, on the left-hand side, is Camp Hopson, one of Newbury's foremost department stores. The store was born in 1921, the offspring of the 'marriage' of two local businesses – one belonging to Alderman Joseph Hopson and the other to Alfred Camp. Inside the present-day department store an oak staircase dating from 1660 to 1680 and contemporary with the building itself can still be found leading from the china department.

Temperance Hall, built in 1875 on the site of a 1722 school. It now houses the Arts Workshop

Almost opposite Camp Hopson's, turn right down Northcroft Lane.

About 50 yards along this road on the right you will find the Temperance Hall, built in 1875 and now housing the town's Arts Workshop. Next to it is the Salvation Army Hall – the inauguration stone of which was laid by Alfred Jackson, mayor of Newbury, on 11 September 1883.

Return to Northbrook Street.

Further along is Newbury Bridge; the building of it was begun in 1769 and finished three years later.

Turn right about 10 yards before the bridge, down a passageway signposted Newbury Lock. Cross over the little metal bridge.

You are now at Newbury Lock, built in 1796 as the first lock on the Kennet and Avon Canal. A broad lock with a brick lock-chamber, its lever-operated ground-paddles, called Jack Cloughs, are the only ones of their kind on the canal.

Beyond this lock, on the left, you will see a large brick building – a block of flats. It was on this site that Town Mills once stood, last used by H. Dolton and Son Ltd to process cereal seed as animal foodstuffs. It closed in 1971 and these modern flats were built in 1981.

Follow the towpath.

On the right, before the swing bridge, you will see the new development of Dolton Mews, built on the site of the old West Mills which was bought by Hovis Ltd in 1921. Later the mill was bought by Windsor and Neate and used as a furniture store. Fire struck in 1965 and the mill was later demolished. The tall building near the swing bridge, now also converted to flats, used to be a grain silo.

Crossing over the swing bridge, continue along the towpath, keeping the canal on your right.

Nos 14, 15 and 16 West Mills (on the left) were once Coxedds Almshouses. Also on the left, on the corner of Kennet Road, are the rather quaint Weavers Cottages.

It is on this stretch of the canal that the South Midland Water Transport Company, one of the few companies to use the canal for transporting goods, unloads its coal three times a year.

About 250 yards further along the canal, on the right-hand side, you will see evidence of the canal's defensive role during the Second World War, in the form of a pillbox. Ballast for building such pillboxes was transported along the canal by Reading firm Collier and Catley Ltd.

Retrace your steps back along the canal towpath. In front of you is St Nicolas church, built over a period of years probably from 1509. Much of the money for the building was provided by Jack of Newbury and his son John, although there were other benefactors too. Several of the town's famous people are buried at St Nicolas, including John Kimber, founder of Kimber's Almshouses (buried 1793).

Just before reaching the swing bridge, at the junction with West Mills, turn right into Kennet Road.

About 50 yards on the left are the John Kimber's almshouses. The original Kimber's Almshouses in Cheap Street were built with money from the will of John Kimber, proved in 1793, and were occupied until 1939 when the new almshouses were built in Kennet Road. The original almshouses were demolished in 1952.

Also on the left, after about another 50 yards, is the Kennet Gospel Hall, built in 1935 for the Christian Brethren, a non-conformist church.

At the end of Kennet Road, turn left into Craven Road.

About 100 yards on the left you will see the imposing Odd Fellow's Hall, built around 1900 as part of the Manchester Union of Odd Fellows, a friendly society.

At the end of Craven Road, turn right into Bartholomew Street.

About 50 yards on the right is Phoenix House, now the premises of James and Cowper chartered accountants, but originally the brewer's house connected to Phoenix Brewery, founded in 1841.

Just about 50 yards further on, again on the right-hand side, are the premises of one of Newbury's oldest surviving companies, the House of Toomer (ironmongers). The firm was established in 1692 by James and Sarah Toomer in Northbrook Street and almost three hundred years later moved to its present site.

Carry on along Bartholomew Street and you will pass over the railway bridge. To the left is Newbury station. A branch line of the Great Western Railway, now called the Thames Line but then known as the Berks and Hants Railway, was built from Reading to Newbury and Newbury to Hungerford and was opened in 1847. The site of a Roman cemetery was discovered here in 1856.

Turn right into Pound Street and almost immediately left into Argyle Road.

You are now in the area of Newbury known as 'The City', one of the prettiest parts of the town and one of the oldest remaining intact – free from the developer's hand. Many of the buildings in Argyle Road are now owned by the Essex Wynter Trust and are used as present-day almshouses. On the right-hand side is the fourteenth-century Bartholomew Manor, a private residence. On the same side further along are cottages which the trust reconditioned in 1929. They were first transformed into almshouses courtesy of Phillip Jemmet in 1670, having started life as a farm building in 1550. The next building on the right, with herringbone bricks, was previously used as the Middlesex Hospital started by Dr Essex Wynter.

On the left, half-way along Argyle Road, is Bartholomew's Hospital, now almshouses. The hospital's foundation date is unknown, but it existed in 1215 in the reign of King John.

Turn left into Derby Road.

On the left-hand side are the older terraced properties of Upper Raymond Almshouses (part of Raymond's Charity) and the more modern bungalows of St Mary's Almshouses. St Mary's Charity was established before the beginning of the seventeenth century to provide almshouses for six poor Newbury women. The original almshouses in Cheap Street were demolished in 1971.

At St John's roundabout, turn left into Newtown Road.

Facing you is the relatively modern structure of St John's church. The original St John's was consecrated in 1860 to serve a new parish created out of parts of the parishes of Newbury and Greenham. But on 10 February 1943 tragedy struck when Newbury was bombed, killing fifteen people, and St John's church was destroyed in the largest fatal casualty incident of the Second World War within the Berkshire County Council area. A temporary church was erected on the site in 1944 and in 1955 the present church was built.

On the left in Newtown Road are the Upper Raymond Almshouses. Just further down the road on the right are the Lower Raymond Almshouses. Raymond's Charity was originally founded in 1676. Three sets of almshouses were built by it over the years. The group of twelve Lower Raymond Almshouses, built in 1796–7, used 40,000 bricks at a total cost of £1,288 8s. 8d.

Opposite the Upper Raymond Almshouses is Fair Close Day Centre, opened in 1967 by HM Queen Elizabeth the Queen Mother as a day centre for the elderly.

Further along Newtown Road, on the left, is the building known as The Litten. It was in the Litten chapel, dating from the fifteenth century, that Jack of Newbury married his master's widow Alice.

Turn right just after Phoenix House into the Eight Bells Shopping Arcade.

Follow this to the small public car park at the back, and in front of you there is a large, modern brick building – Newbury District Council's offices, built in 1982.

Keep to the right and cross over from the district council offices into the open public car park.

It is in this area that the old cattle market was held. Opened in 1873, it was enlarged in 1915 and closed down in 1969.

To the left is the Kennet Centre, a modern shopping mall built on the site of the old Eagle Iron Works which was part of the engineering firm Plenty Ltd.

Further along Market Street, behind the bus station, is the Friends' meeting house (the Quakers). The town's most famous Quaker of the seventeenth century was Oliver Sansom of Boxford, who had several brushes with the law. Just in front of the meeting house, near the old chestnut tree, is a stone marking the site of the old Quaker burial ground.

At the T-junction, turn right into Cheap Street.

About 50 yards on the left are the premises of Newbury Library, opened in 1906 under the Free Libraries Act with the help of £2,000 from American philanthropist Carnegie.

Retrace your steps back to the junction and continue straight along Cheap Street, keeping the Kennet Centre on your left.

After about 100 yards, on the right, you will see the Corn Exchange, which was renovated and re-opened in 1993 after having been closed for several years for safety reasons. It was built in 1862 and in the days of the cattle market was used by traders for selling grain etc. It has also seen a variety of leisure uses.

Almost opposite the Corn Exchange are the premises of W.J. Daniel & Co. Ltd. Charles Daniels took over Albert Jackson's shop, on the same premises, in 1928.

Next on the left is the old Town Hall, otherwise known as Mansion House. Originally built in 1742, it was demolished in 1909 and rebuilt to make a wider route for vehicles.

Facing you is the façade of Beynons, a family department store prominent in the town for over 160 years until it closed in 1990.

Further along, to the right, is the Old Waggon and Horses pub, the earliest reference of which dates back to 1761 when it was granted a licence. In the seventeenth and eighteenth centuries more properties around the market place were public houses than they are now – the White Hart (now Gardner Leader solicitors), the King's Arms (where Dreweatt Neate estate agency is), the Elephant and Castle (also known at one stage as the Three Tuns, but now called the Queen's Hotel) and of course The Hatchet (still a pub).

Garden attached to The Old Waggon & Horses pub in Market Place. The premises are said to be haunted by a drayman who unloads barrels from a boat on the canal

The Next Steps

The following places will be useful to members of the public wishing to find out more about Newbury's history:

Newbury Central Library, Carnegie Road.
Newbury District Museum, The Wharf.
Newbury Tourist Information Centre, The Wharf.
Berkshire Record Office, Shire Hall, Reading. Reader's ticket required.
Kennet and Avon Canal Trust, The Wharf.
Reading Local Studies Library.

Listed below are some of the most useful published books about the history of Newbury.

Astill, G.G., *Historic Towns in Berkshire: An Archaeological Appraisal* (1978).

Balchin, E.W.G.V., *The Country Life Book of the Living History of Britain* (1981).

Bancroft, A., *The New Religious World* (1985).

Barton, D.H., *Memories of the Newbury Bench* (1985).

Beresford, M., *History on the Ground* (1984).

Beresford, M., *New Towns of the Middle Ages (Town Plantation in England, Wales and Gascony)* (1988).

Beresford, M. and Finberg, H.P.R., *English Medieval Boroughs: A Handlist* (1973).

Booker, J., *Thy Chartered Freemen* (1990).

Bradley, D.G., *A Guide to the World's Religions* (1963).

Carter, M., *Archaeology* (1980).

Christian Research Association (formerly Marc Europe), *Prospects for the Nineties* (1991).

Clark, Sir George, *English History (A Survey)* (1971).

Clement, H.A., *The Story of the Ancient World* (1936).

Clew, K.R., *The Kennet and Avon Canal* (1968 and 1973).

Derry, T.K. and Blakeway, M.G., *The Making of Britain* (1968).

Dwyer, G., *Diocese of Portsmouth: Past and Present* (1982).

Dyer, J., *Ancient Britain* (1990).

Falkus, M. and Gillingham, J., *Historical Atlas of Britain* (1981).

Garlick, V.F.M., *The Newbury Scrapbook* (1970).

Gibbs, R.L., *History of St John's Church and Parish Newbury* (1990).

Hadcock, R.N. and Millson, C., *The Story of Newbury* (1990).

Hanbury, H.G. and Yardley, D.C.M., *English Courts of Law* (1979).

Hastings, A., *A History of English Christianity 1920 to 1985* (1986).

Hawkes, J., *The Shell Guide to British Archaeology* (1986).

Hopson, S., *Newbury A Photographic Record 1850 to 1935* (1983).

Judge, C.W., *An Historical Survey of the Didcot, Newbury and Southampton Railway* (1984).

Lindsay Keir, Sir David, *The Constitutional History of Modern Britain since 1485* (1969).

Lockyer, R., *Henry VII* (1983).

Meade, D.M., *The Medieval Church in England* (1988).

Midwinter, H.J., *Newbury Congregational Village Churches* (1919).

Money, W., *The Early History of the Parish of Enborne* (1893).

Money, W., *History of Newbury* (1972).

Paturi, F.R., *Prehistoric Heritage* (1979).

Pearce, G.A.M., *The Parish Church of St Nicolas, Newbury*

Phillips, D., *The Great Road to Bath* (1983).

Phillips, D., *How The Great Western Came to Berkshire, A Railway History 1833 to 1882*

Philpott, Bryan, *The Bombing of Newbury* (1989).

Platt, C., *The English Medieval Town* (1976).

Plucknett, T.F.T., *Concise History of the Common Law* (1956).

Purvis, H., *Talking About Newbury* (1988).

Sands, T.B., *The Didcot, Newbury and Southampton Railway* (1971).

Summers, W.H., *History of the Berkshire, South Oxon, and South Bucks Congregational Churches* (1905).

Walker, Peter N., *The Courts of Law* (1970).

White, R.J., *A Short History of England* (1967).

Wilson, B., *Religious Sects* (1970).

Wood, M., *Domesday (A Search for the Roots of England)* (1986).

Woodward, E.L., *A History of England* (1965).

Wright, C., *The Christian Church* (1982).

Unauthored, *The Lambourn Valley Railway Scrapbook* (1973).

Acknowledgements

I would like to express my thanks to the following: Peter Durrant, Berkshire County Archivist, and his staff; Andrew Lawson, director of Wessex Trust For Archaeology and his staff; staff at Reading Local Studies Library and Newbury Library; David Buxton of Alan Sutton Publishing; Martin Cleveland Photographic Studio; photographer Wayne Pilley; the managing director and photographic staff at Media in Wessex; Rod King, Mary Girdler, Janne Dawson and the Howell family for proofreading, and all the many other individuals and companies who helped. Particular thanks must go to Newbury Museum curator Tony Higgott, assistant curator Paul Cannon and all the museum staff, without whom this book would never have got off the ground.

NB All dates given in this book are in Old Style.

Picture Credits

I would like to acknowledge the following for their kind permission to reproduce illustrations: Berkshire County Records Office (pp. 16, 21 (top), 28, 55), Buxworth Steam Group (p. 101), Courtyard Antiques (p. 27), Gordon Edwards (p. 90), *Evening Post*, Reading (pp.11, 98), John Gould (pp. 89, 112 (top)), Jack Hole/Bert Dennis (pp. 80, 81), Bob Naylor/Media in Wessex (p. 67), Newbury Library (pp. 59, 100, 104, 112 (bottom)), Newbury Museum (pp. 4, 69, 73, 79, 86, 97), Newbury Museum/Martin Cleveland Photographic Studio (pp. 5, 6, 13, 26, 88), Newbury Museum/Wayne Pilley (pp. 21 (bottom), 22, 29, 36 (bottom), 47, 51, 54, 58 (bottom), 60, 64, 65, 70, 76, 77, 78), David Pilgrim (pp. 42, 50, 107), Wayne Pilley (p. 3), Plenty Ltd (pp. 43, 93), Reading Local Studies Library (pp. 12, 32 (top), 96 (top), 105), St Mary's Parochial Church Council (p. 31), PC David Stubbs (p. 96 (bottom)), Susan Tolman (pp. 11, 19, 32 (bottom), 36 (top), 56, 58 (top), 72, 109, 114, 118), United Reformed Church (pp. 85, 103), Nicholas Vine (p. 91).

Index